W9-DFM-565

03/24
STAND PRICE
$ 5.00

THE
TIP
OF THE
ICEBERG

THE
TIP
OF THE
ICEBERG

THE UNKNOWN TRUTH BEHIND
INDIA'S START-UPS

SUVEEN SINHA

PORTFOLIO
PENGUIN

PORTFOLIO

USA | Canada | UK | Ireland | Australia
New Zealand | India | South Africa | China

Portfolio is part of the Penguin Random House group of companies
whose addresses can be found at global.penguinrandomhouse.com

Published by Penguin Random House India Pvt. Ltd
7th Floor, Infinity Tower C, DLF Cyber City,
Gurgaon 122 002, Haryana, India

First published in Portfolio by Penguin Random House India 2016

Copyright © Suveen Sinha 2016

All rights reserved

10 9 8 7 6 5 4 3 2 1

The views and opinions expressed in this book are the author's own and the
facts are as reported by him, which have been verified to the extent possible,
and the publishers are not in any way liable for the same.

ISBN 9780670088331

Typeset in Sabon by Manipal Digital Systems, Manipal
Printed at Replika Press Pvt. Ltd, India

This book is sold subject to the condition that it shall not, by way of trade
or otherwise, be lent, resold, hired out, or otherwise circulated without the
publisher's prior consent in any form of binding or cover other than that in
which it is published and without a similar condition including this
condition being imposed on the subsequent purchaser.

www.penguinbooksindia.com

To Neha and Sahir,
without whose constant involvement, this book could have
been done a lot sooner (but life would have been a lot less fun);

to Anish,
without whom this book could not have been done;

and, to all those who wander without being lost:
the characters, and the real writers, of this book

'All that is gold does not glitter,
Not all those who wander are lost;
The old that is strong does not wither,
Deep roots are not reached by the frost.'

—J.R.R. Tolkien, *The Fellowship of the Ring*

Contents

The Cast

AVNISH BAJAJ: Baazee, Matrix Partners India

BHAVISH AGGARWAL: OlaCabs

DEVITA SARAF: Vu Technologies

DHIRAJ RAJARAM: Mu Sigma

HARISH BAHL: Smile Group

KUNAL BAHL: Snapdeal

MANMOHAN AGARWAL AND NITIN AGARWAL: Yebhi

PEARL UPPAL: FashionAndYou

PHANINDRA SAMA: redBus

RADHIKA GHAI AGGARWAL: ShopClues

RAHUL YADAV: Housing.com

SHASHANK N.D.: Practo

SUCHI MUKHERJEE: LimeRoad

VIJAY SHEKHAR SHARMA: Paytm

YOGENDRA VASUPAL: Stayzilla

Prologue

Rahul Yadav tries to be polite, in the manner of someone who needs to try. Our conversation has just begun, and an early question is the standard, break-the-ice routine: How did it all begin?

'The realization that this . . . father in merchant navy . . .' he trails off, breaks eye contact to look to his right, a reluctant half-smile playing on his lips. The slight note of exasperation is unmistakable. He has narrated the story too many times already.

'Nowadays I get bored. I think I should make a video of it,' he says, like a petulant child who is being careful because he is talking to the uncle who is respected by the family.

The video idea brightens him up. 'Yeah, that will be efficient. I can try to cover everything in it. I skip things and try to keep it short because I have to repeat.'

Presently, though, he moves on to narrate his story in a perfunctory sort of way, without relish. He probably does it to get it out of the way and get to the point, which is also his plan to run the world.

It is a simple plan—all it will take is about fifty smart people. Going by the vibes, I have little chance of being included in that group, but I do have the opportunity to ask what he thinks is wrong with the way the world is run today.

It is a subject he likes talking about. His broad face, with wide cheekbones, and bordered on top by a mop of smooth black hair, looks suddenly animated. His speech, though it cannot be described as crisp English with flawless grammar, sounds intense with purpose.

The world, believes this twenty-six-year-old, is run by very incapable people. From an early age he has been baffled about why we cannot do things better. He believes he has to take the initiative to set them right. Look at energy, he says. Instead of finding better, sustainable and less polluting sources, all we have done is burned oil and 'almost fucked up the planet'.

Food management is no better. Every time Rahul Yadav eats, he feels stressed because what he eats is bound to make him fat. Our staples were probably relevant twenty years ago, when humans spent more energy doing physical work.

The state of education troubles Rahul Yadav even more. In his assessment, formal education used to be two or three decades behind what was going on in the real world. But of late technology has been changing every two or three years, leaving education several generations behind. And nobody really wants to change the education system because it will have to be changed in real time, which would be like having to repair a moving car as education cannot be on pause. It has to go on.

'It is, again, the incapability of these people. Look around, there are examples and examples.'

Which of those can or will be fixed by Housing.com? That's the realty company Rahul set up in June 2012, having left the Indian Institute of Technology, Bombay, the previous year, when he still had a year to go. Eleven of his friends from the institute joined him later, after completing their course. The company started as Housing.co.in. It became Housing.com a year later, after they bought the domain name from 'some US guy' for a million dollars.

That—a start-up spending such money to buy its domain name—was unheard of in India. But Rahul believes there is a lot in a name, as it conveys purpose. He has the name On Time in mind for a real estate brokers' club he wants to set up. The name is appropriate, he says, as brokers are always late to meetings.

Rahul's company can afford to spend that amount on a domain name because it has raised $121 million from the investors SoftBank, Nexus Ventures, Helion Ventures, and Falcon Edge.

But there is more to Housing.com than its bank balance. It has caused an upheaval in the real estate sector by adding the element of transparency to a most opaque business. It verifies the properties it lists, posts their photographs, and gives the visitor a virtual tour. It insists on giving the exact location—something that is seen as extremely important in anyone's decision to buy a house, but also something that is seldom described.

'It is not gonna end with Housing.com; there is going to be much more. I believe this earth is a big company. And these governments and financial institutions are its board and management. They are incapable. That's why it's a big, inefficient company. We should just take over and correct it.'

Who is we?

'The people who are capable, the next generation, my team and the vectors that are coming out of me. I believe the world can be run by just fifty smart people, and nobody will have a problem. Everything will be so good. One guy can solve the entire travel problem, one guy can solve the entire food problem, one guy can solve the housing problem.'

Those guys will be given a free run. 'Right now, most of the world's companies are doing the same thing—wasting time, wasting human life.'

Rahul does not think any of this is too radical. If anything, it will be readily embraced by those who suffer because of dumb decisions taken by the earth's management. For instance, in Mumbai people travel in local trains for hours to get to work and then go back home at the end of the day. They don't get much time with the family or in bed because the struggle begins again early the next day.

'We have enough resources. We have been given a planet. This management-layer-over-management-layer-over-management-layer has become complex. What's going on? Very few people can run the whole world so that everyone can enjoy the resources that we have on this planet. It is just that there are incapable managers.'

By this time, Rahul Yadav is speaking rapidly, almost breathlessly, as if exasperated with the whole world and not just with me. And then, just like that, he chooses to talk about his company's area.

All the houses in Mumbai are the same: boxes, boxes and boxes. There is no infrastructure. Nobody is thinking of improving the houses or redesigning them at a fundamental level. A third of your life is spent in bed, but the bed has remained the same over the years.

In reality—and Rahul Yadav sounds sure of this—all that people want is happiness. Nobody wants to travel. Nobody wants to do anything. They just want happiness. Which comes in two parts: instant happiness and investment for future happiness. But people these days are only investing for future happiness, sacrificing the instant kind. 'I don't care about these things. I keep the weight of instant happiness a lot higher.'

What gives him happiness?

'Any action. I am always happy.'

But he does not really look happy.

'I don't smile so that the other guy doesn't think I am mad. The facial expression is always normal. But internally there is extreme joy and happiness.'

Isn't he lucky?

No, he is just smart. 'You just have to be smart and understand the world, so that you can enjoy anything. Even if there is an event that people call sad or bad, I find it really exciting.'

~

Devita Saraf, too, wants to change the world, but she would rather do it in her petite, warm, friendly, well-dressed, well-groomed, sweet way, with easy chuckles. And she has little time for the IIT types who think they are God's gift to mankind.

There was one she had hired at Vu Technologies—Vu is pronounced 'view'—the company she started in 2006, when she was just twenty-four, to make luxury television sets. She had personally trained him. Everything went well for a while. The kid was bright, perhaps a tad too bright. One day he complained that he was not learning anymore and therefore losing interest in his work.

'Go,' Devita told him. 'This is not a college, you are not paying fees, I am paying you a salary.'

He went away and Devita still has not understood his approach to life, and that of many others of his ilk. To her, this constant talk of learning is nonsense. Do a job of responsibility, whether in your own company or someone else's, and learning will come. Some day she would like to tell him: '*Beta*, you are so clueless. I don't think any girl wants you. You consider yourself so smart, but if your mother still has to find a wife for you, consider yourself a failure.'

What about the start-up culture? The unbathed, unwashed glamour of being disorganized and unshaven? 'Yikes! Nonsense! I am a luxury technology company. If I have people coming in wearing jeans and slogan T-shirts, you are not going to buy my product. I don't need my people to dress like *jhalla*s just to look cool. In any case, Indian men look terrible in casuals. Even my peon is well-dressed. What our country needs is people who have confidence inside and out, not some moron who has just rolled out of bed. I am not putting up bunkers in office for people to sleep in. We work Monday to Saturday, 10 a.m. to 6.30 p.m. Beyond that, what you do is your problem.'

Monday to Saturday, 10 a.m. to 6.30 p.m., if you turn up wearing jeans or a sleeveless top, you pay a fine of Rs 500. If you show up with a stubble, you will have to go home, shave, and return. If you are late, you will have to take the day off.

There is one thing, though, that she dislikes more than the hoodie-wearing-I'm-not-learning-anymore kind. That is, the children of wealthy businessmen, the second or third generation of business families who just waste their time. Both girls and boys. In fact, she finds that half of those boys are just like girls. All they care about is a fancy social life which they can show off.

'Guys are the new girls. They are like, okay, let me have a dinner party for my friends'—here she acquires a false, mocking voice. 'Talking to them is like talking to a girl. They know brands, fashion, and handbags. People ask me why I'm not married. I say because I don't want a wife. Where are the men?'

She cannot understand the other type either, the kind that does not want to join their father's business because they find it dull and full of old people. Instead of finding something meaningful in that, or maybe creating something new, they choose to go to New York and slog it out in some stupid job because that gives them the chance to think: 'It's so me.'

Devita finds it sad. 'People who have the resources, foreign education, and all the support, their life is all about where they went on vacation and which wine they drank.'

It is delicious to hear her take off like that on children of business families. She is one.

~

'How did you parents react when you said you were going to set up your own company?'

This is one question I asked each of the dozens of entrepreneurs I met for this book. The answers were invariably interesting. Suchi Mukherjee's mother thought setting up LimeRoad spelled the end of her thus-far glittering career. Bhavish Aggarwal's father did not speak to him for months because he thought his computer engineer son, by setting up OlaCabs, had become a travel agent.

But Rahul Yadav's answer will always linger on in my memory. For it amuses and troubles in equal measure.

'I have not yet told them.' Heck, he has not even told them he dropped out of IIT.

Not told them that you dropped out?

'Yeah.'

And they do not know you have set up a company?

'They know I am doing something on my own. But no idea what, exactly.'

How is that possible?

'If you tell them, they will eat your brain.'

Rahul's dad was in the merchant navy, his mom a homemaker. They live in Khairthal, a tiny speck in the Alwar district of Rajasthan, at the northern end of the Aravalli mountain range. They are simple people who read the local Hindi newspaper. Rahul has an older sister who is married and lives in a world far removed from the Internet. He also has a younger brother who may have some idea about what Rahul is up to because he is on Facebook.

Curiously, Rahul's Facebook profile does not mention any family. But it was an uncle who may have unintentionally changed the course of Rahul's life by making a caustic comment when he stood twentieth among thirty students in class ten. The comment stung. Two years later, Rahul topped the state in the class twelve exams in the physics-chemistry-maths stream.

The natural course from there on took him to IIT, and in 2007 he found himself in Powai, one of Mumbai's few picturesque areas that is home to IIT Bombay. He ended up studying metallurgy, a far cry from the glamour of computer science, but he shone especially in campus politics, getting himself elected as secretary of the students' association. During that election campaign he realized there was a need to reference old examination papers and created exambaba.com, an online bank of question papers. The institute later shut it down. But the lesson was indelible: 'If you need something and it does not exist, build it yourself.'

In their final year, Rahul and his friends imagined themselves living outside the campus once their course ended. But they found their imagination muddied by the difficulty of finding a house, the general intransigence of brokers, and the high commissions they charged. So they decided to build a solution.

Getting the first tranche of money was not that difficult. It was a small amount raised from their IIT seniors. The leader of the angel pack was Zishaan Hayath, who had graduated in 2005. Hayath runs toppr.com, an online preparation platform for entrance examinations, and Powai Lake Ventures.

Using this money, Rahul and friends began to build the site on which those looking for a house could actually see real, good quality photographs of the properties on offer.

They could also take a virtual, three-dimensional tour of the properties. The data was verified, as was the location.

Sounds simple and sensible, right? Yet nobody had done it before, while Housing.com, with its DNA of IIT techies, kept adding features.

That was the easy part. Raising further rounds of investment, which would typically come from venture capitalist firms, proved tricky. 'I got rejected by 97–98 per cent of the VCs.' Rahul had made multiple rounds of nearly every one of the VCs in town, encouraged by the advice of a friend: 'Rahul, if you want a girlfriend, you need to go out and party. If you need investment, you cannot just sit back and say you have already met five VCs. *Lakshmi khud chal kar nahi aayegi*.' And so Rahul knocked on more VCs' doors.

It took time. Some liked his company's idea but not the numbers. Some liked both, but not him. And so it went on. Eventually, those that did invest in the company were among the best in the business. SoftBank's $90 million in December 2014, valuing the company at $250 million, established Housing.com as one of the hottest start-ups in the country.

Having focused on developing the product for two-and-a-half years, Housing.com spent some of its ample cash on a massive advertising and promotion campaign, reportedly at a cost of Rs 120 crore. No other three-year-old company spends this kind of money on advertising. It grew its footprint from twenty cities in 2014 to 100 by the end of May 2015.

～

It had been three years since Devita Saraf had joined her father, Rajkumar's Zenith Computers as director of marketing. As usual, they were travelling together to work. (She still insists on it because that's when she can 'chew his brain'.)

That morning the traffic on the Bandra flyover was its usual cheek-to-jowl. But Devita barely noticed the traffic. She was busy talking to her father about her bright idea of marrying high technology with luxury in a television set. She was excited. Suddenly, she stopped in mid-speech; her father had just said something.

It took her a second to realize what. How would she like to start this business and take charge of it? Devita was just twenty-four. She took her time to say yes . . . About three seconds.

Neither father nor daughter was surprised by what the other had said. One day it had to come to this. The seeds were sown in the way Rajkumar Saraf and wife, Vijayrani, had chosen to bring up their little girl.

From an early age, Devita had learned to speak her mind and make clear choices. For instance, there was this NASSCOM conference in Hyderabad that looked really interesting. And there was this class eleven accounts exam the same day that looked really stupid in comparison. She could have passed it with her eyes closed; most of the stuff she had studied in classes nine and ten. But she would learn much more in Hyderabad.

Vijayrani, a post-graduate from the Delhi School of Economics, was not sure it was right of her daughter to want to skip the exam. Academics were important to the mother. But the father, as Marwari a businessman as they come, did not have a moment's hesitation in telling Devita to book her tickets. They would find a solution to the skipped exam later.

'I think of exams as an insult to my intelligence,' says Devita. Her intelligence is something she has always been proud of. It comes certified: she is a member of the international high IQ society, Mensa.

It occurred to her to take the Mensa test when she went to the United States to study in 1999–2000. When she was in school, she once got into a bit of a situation with one of her teachers. The teacher had given her just 12 per cent marks on a test. Devita had told the teacher to keep the marks. 'If you think you are so smart, join the Mensa,' the teacher had shot back sarcastically.

Devita scored 86 per cent marks in the next test, but the Mensa remark stayed with her. She cracked the Mensa while in the US. She would have loved to tell her teacher about it but—and this makes her sad—the teacher had died by that time.

~

When we spoke, on 20 March 2015, Rahul Yadav was not in the news for trying to take the world by the wheel. He was for taking on the boys who man the India office of Sequoia Capital, one of the more formidable VC firms in the country. Sequoia had neatly cleaved the start-up and entrepreneur community. It is difficult to take names, but half the people seemed to think that Sequoia had met its comeuppance and the other half that Rahul Yadav was a raving lunatic.

Both parties agreed, though, that Rahul could have been more careful in his choice of words. This is what he had posted to Shailendra Singh, managing director of Sequoia Capital, on Quora, the popular social platform that follows a question-and-answer format, on Friday, 6 March 2015, at 7.39 p.m. The subject line was: 'Last Straw'.

Dude,
    I've been humble to you guys even after inhuman and unethical things that you've done with Housing in the past.
    You did the same inhuman and unethical things with large number of entrepreneurs including Ola, TFS, Flipkart, Dexetra and many more . . .

Now I just came to know you personally are completely after Housing's employees and are brainwashing them to open some stupid incubation.

If you don't stop messing around with me, directly or even indirectly, I will vacate the best of your firm.

Also, this mark the beginning of the end of Sequoia Cap in India.

Try me

Enjoy Holi!
Cheers,
Rahul

Shailendra Singh's response, on Quora again, was five times as long. He sounded hurt. But he chose to put out the facts. Sequoia was expanding its analyst pool to include younger team members who had start-up experience. It had evaluated over 100 candidates from multiple companies and geographies. Singh had personally met with about a dozen of them, including two Housing.com employees. One of them was made an offer and decided to take it.

Singh went on to talk about the sense of community and professionalism among entrepreneurs, investors and employees in Silicon Valley. He had met Rahul in person just once, and was happy to hear all the good things being spoken about his company.

Sequoia, Singh continued, was trusted by some of the best and brightest entrepreneurs, not just to be in their cap table, but also to help set the direction for their companies. 'We take our role very seriously, and we are deeply committed to our portfolio companies and their teams. Honestly, we have neither time nor intention to do anything else, let alone target a company we have no ownership in.'

For all of Rahul's rakish charm, Singh's was the more mature and cultured post.

But not everyone agreed with everything that Singh had written. According to a well-regarded angel investor, Rahul Yadav was just the child who had said out loud that the emperor was naked, that he was not wearing new clothes. Sachin Bansal, one of the two founders of Flipkart, the country's biggest start-up success, tweeted: 'Sequoia isn't an investor with us. I would just say I'm glad to have it that way.'

To another successful entrepreneur, one who likes to be aloof and quiet, the entire episode was *paagalpan* (madness). *'Kaam nahi hai kya ?'* he wondered. (Do people have no work to do?')

To Rahul, it was all in a day's work. 'Nothing happened as such. For me it is just a regular days' event. It just went public. I deal with such things every day. And my responses are equally strong on a regular basis. Just went public because I think there were . . . yes, it did cross a certain limit, that's why. Otherwise for me it is very regular.'

How could it be regular? He had written about inhuman things.

'I'm not going to go into the details about Sequoia.'

The gossip mill was abuzz. Some said Yadav was about to be sacked as the CEO of Housing.com. Others wondered if he had a private jet—figure out the connection if you can. Certainly this paagalpan would have distracted him from the *kaam*?

No, not Rahul Yadav. 'It is a simple thing. We can run the whole planet, all the countries.'

So why was he so upset with Sequoia? All that it had tried to do was to poach a couple of his people.

'I'll give you an example. Let's say in class you have good relations with someone and bad relations with someone else. If the friend tears a page out of your notebook, you will be fine with it. But if the other one tries to touch your notebook, you will slap him.'

Rahul's company's terms with Sequoia may have been frozen when, as part of his efforts to raise Series A funding—the stage after the seed and angel rounds, when the big-ass investors come in—Rahul had 'an interesting conversation' with the firm.

Forty days after we spoke, Rahul Yadav was slapping his investors and board members. And apologizing.

~

Devita likes to be independent and make her own decisions. But she is glad for what she has got. She lives with her parents and does not need to worry about her next meal. There is a maid to cook for her, another to clean her home, and the driver to take her wherever she wants to go in a comfortable car.

She could have opted to marry someone from the Sarafs' social circle, another business family scion, and spent her time doing a bit of CSR. But she likes the hustle and bustle that Vu puts her through. For instance, she went to the Kochi Biennale and signed up as a sponsor. Her mother got to know of this only two days before the event began, when Devita had told the driver to come at a certain hour to take her to the airport. At the time we met, her favourite story was about this Malayali guy writing the middle name of Vu Luxury Television as Lexury.

It was the same when she was with Zenith. Always in the thick of things. She was the point person for Zenith's work with Microsoft and Intel. She visited the MIT Media Lab and Intel's and Apple's innovation labs to see the new product development approach using human factors. She used to interact with customers, too, and saw the changes in young

Indians. She saw that they were falling for a lifestyle approach and decided to apply the new product development approach to create a new kind of television.

Vu's television sets marry the best of other industries like hospitality, fashion and entertainment. They are innovative and can also be enjoyed by the common people, not justgeeks. That the price can be as high as Rs 9 lakh for an 85-inch unit is another matter.

Unlike the other entrepreneurs you will meet in this book, Devita did not have to grapple with the issue of funding. Bootstrapping, seed and angel funding, Series A, B and C, etc. are vague concepts to her. Vu is a separate company, but its veins throb with Zenith's blood. It is funded by the Saraf family. It has its own team, but some key people came over from Zenith.

Vu did not have to worry about infrastructure. It operates out of a spacious, three-floor office in a Mumbai building that bears its name at the front gate. 'The systems and processes are there. But when I brought forward my good ideas, I was also very cost conscious. It was not like I was taking my father's money and burning it up . . . The base was there, but creating the magic, creating what's new, is what I added.'

That idea, that magic was the key for her. It was not as though she thought of turning entrepreneur because it was the cool thing to do. It so happened that the idea grabbed her and brought her to Vu.

'I didn't think I would start my own business. It was an opportunity that came: "Let's do a high-end television brand."' In fact, Vu first started as a project within Zenith before it was branched out, once the brand took off.

~

Dear board members and investors, I don't think you guys are intellectually capable enough to have any sensible discussion anymore. This is something which I not just believe but can prove on your faces also!

I had calculated long back (by taking avg life expectancy minus avg sleeping hrs) that I only have ~3L (hours) in my life. ~3L hrs are certainly not much to waste with you guys!

Hence resigning from the position of Directorship, Chairmanship and the CEO position of the company. I'm available for the next 7 days to help in the transition. Won't give more time after that. So please be efficient in this duration.

Cheers,
Rahul

Dated 30 April 2015, the email above is what Rahul Yadav wrote to Housing.com's board. Of course, it got leaked and quickly spread all over the news and social media. Controversy's child had struck again.

Deepinder Goyal, who set up and runs the very successful start-up Zomato, tweeted: 'Housing is what happens when investors leave founders with little skin in the game. Especially, 20-year-old founders with nothing to lose.'

Early in the morning on 5 May, Rahul and the board—SoftBank's Jonathan Bullock, along with representatives of Nexus and Helion—went into a meeting at law firm AZB and partners' office at Mumbai's Nariman Point. The meeting went on long after its scheduled close—they moved to a second conference room after a while and later to a third.

After seven hours or so, they came out smiling. Rahul had rescinded his resignation, with an apology. 'After some frank and healthy discussions with the board I have agreed to withdraw my resignation and I apologize for my unacceptable comments about the board members. I look forward to staying on at Housing as CEO and building an even greater company, while working in full harmony with the board.' In an email to Housing.com employees, he said: 'Was just a usual day at Housing, I am still your CEO. Have fun.'

Running the company was now going to become serious business, though. Considerable give and take seemed to have happened at the board meeting. It will not be wrong to say that Rahul was playing his resignation as a card. And this time he won. The board did not want to let him go; after all, the young man was behind all the happy disruption the start-up has caused in real estate.

For his part, Rahul finally agreed to behave like the CEO of a company. Now he would seek the board's consent for big decisions, unlike earlier when he would buy a domain name without discussing it with the board. He tweeted after the board meeting that it was like going back to school. Presumably he would be learning stuff.

Or maybe not. He threw the ensuing AGM of the company into a tizzy by announcing that he was distributing his 4.57 per cent equity in the company among the employees. The board was as surprised, though not so pleasantly as the employees, who stood to receive about a year's salary in stocks. Of course, loyalty to the young CEO would be a small and natural concession.

This may have been as calculated a decision as the resignation, only with higher stakes. It made Rahul an instant hero among the employees of Housing.com as well as those working at other start-ups. This young man, the message went, was not in it for the money but only to realize his vision of solving a problem that has perhaps not been solved anywhere in the world.

For good measure, Rahul also threw bait in Zomato founder, Deepinder Goyal's direction, whom he disparages as a restaurant menu scanner, and OlaCabs founder Bhavish

Aggarwal, whom he admires, challenging them to follow
suit and give up their stakes. Goyal responded with a tweet:
'Aww. So cute!'

~

As Devita Saraf was walking me to her cabin, she stopped for
a moment to look at a colleague's computer screen. This was
November 2014 and the colleague, Vinod, who looked after
Vu's social media presence, was planning a Christmas offer
and calling it 'Vu's Santastic Offer'. In an instant, Devita told
him to go ahead.

That is how quick her decisions are.

However, what about the view outside Vu? She wrote for
the *Wall Street Journal* for two years. Surely, her mind should
be wandering in other directions too?

'I want to become the prime minister. But I would choose
to be the prime minister of a different country.'

By that she does not mean another country, but a changed
India. 'Young Indians do not spend enough time thinking
about leadership. We think the topper of the class should be
the leader. That is stupid because toppers are loners. It's like
making Sachin Tendulkar the captain—bad for everyone.
Instead of going on social media and just complaining, you
should be in a position to make a change.'

She halts in her tracks as I point out that it is only
the leader of the largest political party in the Lok Sabha
who becomes the prime minister. Had she given it serious
thought?

'Yes, but my family thinks politics is dirty. Bombay people
don't think well of politics. They are politically agnostic. My
mother is originally from Uttar Pradesh and says even the
rickshaw puller in Uttar Pradesh and Bihar is interested in
politics and knows all the ministers. In Bombay, they know

no one beyond the chief minister.' (Some not even that much, as Alia Bhatt showed on *Koffee with Karan*.)

Right now, Devita has no time for politics anyway. Her hands are full as Vu has grown steadily from zero to Rs 100 crore in revenue over eight years. Rs 40 crore have been sunk into it as investment, including the cost of establishment .

But once Vu crosses Rs 500 crore in revenue, she would like to take a deep breath and think about what to do next. There is a sliver of a chance it might be cars. But Vu would look at cars very differently. 'I hate reverse parking. The wheels turn only about 45 degrees or so. In a trolley, they move 360. Why can't the wheels of a car move 360 degrees?'

She has other questions. Why can't the driver's seat be in the centre, instead of always to the right or left? Why does a car need a front and a back and wheels on the side? Why can't cars be modular? Why can't I add seats as my family grows? Why do I need a front passenger seat in a Mercedes? Nobody sits in it, ever. Can I have a laptop table in its place?

Basic stuff, really, though it will need enormous investment and nous. That might make it as tough as becoming the leader of the largest party in the Lok Sabha.

'I don't know how I will go about becoming the prime minister,' Devita is thoughtful again. 'Laws can be changed. The Constitution can be amended. It was not faxed from Heaven. By the time I am sixty or seventy I'm sure things will change.'

~

'Ye mote Gururaj uncle har chhoti cheez par article kyu likh dete hain.'

The moment you saw this comment on a column by Ravi Gururaj on yourstory.com, you knew a backlash was round

the corner. Not so much because of what was said but because
of who said it: Rahul Yadav.

That is not to say that the 'mote uncle' comment was
great. But it was not really a crime. In fact, it would be quite
funny if it had been made by a naughty child who is otherwise
so bright and interesting that you want to indulge him. Which
is somewhat the case here, though, at twenty-six, Rahul is no
child.

Gururaj, chairman of NASSCOM's Product Council, the
writer of that column, will be the first to admit that he cannot be
called thin. He had written the column about a supposed social
media spat between Snapdeal's Rohit Bansal and Flipkart's
Sachin Bansal. Rohit was perceived as saying in a newspaper
article that India did not have enough good programmers. Sachin
took a dig at him, suggesting that the fault lay in Snapdeal and
not in the country's programming community.

Rahul's was the first comment on Gururaj's article. Others
followed quickly, saying all he wanted was cheap publicity.
Publicity? By trying to make fun of Gururaj? Come on. There
are other ways to earn publicity; Rahul knows some of them.
Almost inevitably, an article appeared in *ET Panache* about
how Gururaj was large-hearted enough to ignore Rahul's
comment. What was he going to do? Sue? Equally inevitably,
Alok Kejriwal, an early entrepreneur, jumped to Gururaj's
side to say how much he loved him for his 'stature and
presence and depth'.

Now, Kejriwal and Rahul Yadav have a bit of a shared
background. Kejriwal had clicked pictures of two Housing.com
hoardings and posted them online. According to him, the
positioning of the hoardings was not right for getting the
maximum return on marketing expenses; that Housing.com's
founders were dumb to do it.

Rahul responded with a detailed explanation of how the
positioning was just right. Of course, in retort he called Kejriwal's

argument dumb. For good measure, according to newspaper reports, some people played around with Kejriwal's Wikipedia page to edit his location and showed him as living under two Housing.com hoardings.

Kejriwal waited for his chance, which came when Yadav resigned—the first time. People who make fun of other people's houses can't live in their own, he posted. He also posted a PowerPoint presentation, for Rahul, on how to write emails.

Still okay. Nobody died. They were all just boys having fun (though Kejriwal, who was born in 1968 and likes to call himself 'Rodinhood', is less young). Who hasn't done it in college and hostel? With the Internet start-up revolution, all the world is a boys' hostel.

But one of those boys, Rahul Yadav, has now disappeared, having finally left Housing.com in early July 2015.

Fine, he is cheeky, and at times irritating. He likes to troll people. But he is not just that. The sadness of his oust was captured in all its delicate sensitivity by Haresh Chawla, an early investor in Housing.com, in a column for the website foundingfuel.com. He brought out Rahul's personality in all its complexity: a shy, socially-awkward, brilliant soul driven to pain and distraction because he was forced to ride the tiger of investor money.

~

Rahul Yadav and Devita Saraf are two faces of the entrepreneurship revolution that has engulfed India. They come from very different worlds. Yadav is brazen and cussed where Saraf is colour-coordinated and comely. But, however different, they are both fish in the same pond, peas in the same pod. And between them expands the vast and wonderful rainbow of start-ups and entrepreneurs that has space for every hue.

The brightest hue in there is that of Flipkart founders Sachin Bansal and Binny Bansal. They may never have spoken to each other had it not been for their separate failures to complete their projects in time at IIT Delhi.

The Bansals, who are not related, declined to talk to me for this book, though Sachin offered to push it on Flipkart. In fact, Dhiraj Rajaram, founder and CEO of Mu Sigma, probably the most special start-up to come out of India, wrote to Sachin that he and Binny should participate in it. But Sachin wrote to Dhiraj repeating what he had written to me: he just did not have the time for it.

That is understandable. Flipkart has been growing at breakneck speed. It has turned fundraising into an art form, pushing its valuation, at one time, to as much as $15 billion. Underlying that valuation is its ever-increasing gross merchandise value. That is the total value of goods sold on the online marketplace calculated on MRP, without factoring in discounts. At the time this book was being written, Flipkart was chasing $10 billion in annual GMV. That would be two-and-a-half times the $4 billion it clocked in 2014–15 and ten times the previous year's figure of $1 billion.

Going by the 2014 festival season when, for the first time, online shopping overshadowed offline buying, Flipkart should get to the $10 billion mark. Hot in its pursuit, though perhaps in some ways behind, would be the other online marketplace stars such as Snapdeal and One97 Communication's Paytm, and also the much older and established offline retailer, Future Group.

Fortunately, the Bansals of Flipkart have given enough interviews for us to know that they both studied at the same school, DAV College, Chandigarh—a year apart. Sachin had been senior to Binny; neither had spoken to the other until one desolate summer in Delhi.

At IIT, if you do not finish your project during a semester, you had better stay on campus during summer break to finish it. One semester, Sachin was working on what he described in a television interview as a very small part of a very small project for the Indian navy. He could not finish it and had to stay on during the summer.

Most of the other students had gone away, leaving those left behind to strike new friendships with one another. Binny Bansal was also around. He had not completed his project to build an optimizing tool in hardware for image-processing software for automotive applications such as the self-driving car. Both were from the same city. Both were doing computer science. They got talking and haven't stopped since.

The idea of starting a company had not occurred to either while they were at IIT. The system around them certainly did not encourage any such thoughts. Everybody was either in a race to find a job or crack the CAT, or go overseas for higher studies. Sachin was clear he did not want to go abroad, either for a job or to study. He did not want to go too far from his parents.

After graduating from IIT in 2005, he joined Techspan for a few months before moving to Amazon Web Services in January 2006. After a year, once he had a strong footing there, he pulled in Binny, who was working at Sarnoff. Now that they were both in the same office in Bangalore, the hotbed of start-ups, they got talking again. Exactly nine months after Binny joined AWS, both left in September 2007 and started Flipkart.

But the story of entrepreneurship in India started much before that. The Infosys IPO of 1991 was an early high watermark. However, the modern entrepreneurs, most of whom dabble heavily in technology, have set new standards with their appetite for risk and sense of adventure. Their tribe is large and ever increasing.

Kunal Bahl of Snapdeal, Vijay Shekhar Sharma of Paytm, Shashank N.D. of Practo and Yogendra Vasupal of Stayzilla were dreaming even while Sachin and Binny were first toiling away at AWS and then trying to make people buy books online. Avnish Bajaj had already become a big fish in a small pond when he sold Baazee, the company he co-founded, to eBay in 2004.

The millennial entrepreneurs are different from the ones that came before. The earlier generation of entrepreneurs, such as N.R. Narayana Murthy of Infosys and Azim Premji of Wipro, adopted technologies developed outside India and serviced global companies. The new entrepreneurs are creating their own products and technologies, their aspirations fuelled by Internet and mobile applications. They are also confident of holding their own against the world.

In part that could be because they are servicing the Indian market, where a Bansal beats a Bezos. But the Indian market is not a confinement. Zomato has acquired companies in several countries. As I write, the culture of entrepreneurship is sweeping across not just Bangalore but also Mumbai, the National Capital Region, Pune, Chandigarh, Hyderabad and many more towns and cities across India. As for the entrepreneurs, they also come from all over; from the poor pockets of Rajasthan as well as from the posh corporations in the UK and US, having left their high-profile careers there.

The new entrepreneurs have shown a trenchant keenness to fund the dreams of other entrepreneurs—something Murthy and Premji started doing much later in their careers. There is a long list of start-ups being funded by founders of other start-ups. Some like Avnish Bajaj have gone ahead and become venture capitalists.

Naturally, it has been raining money on start-ups. Newspaper headlines about less-known companies raising Rs 100 crore have become mundane. In part it is thanks to the opportunity the big fund houses missed in China, where Alibaba, TenCent and Baidu had become quite costly by the time the VCs got the chance to wet their beak. It took them time to believe that such large companies could come out of China so quickly. Now they do not want to miss the India opportunity.

Hedge funds, investment firms and asset managers have pumped $3.8 billion into twenty-six Indian tech start-ups since the beginning of 2014, according to data compiled by Bangalore-based Tracxn. At least seven Indian technology start-ups—Flipkart, Snapdeal, OlaCabs, Paytm, Mu Sigma, ShopClues and Zomato—have become unicorns. That's what they call start-ups that get valued at more than a billion dollars.

There is also the flip side, as there is to every story. Globally, only about 10 per cent of start-ups survive, and they are usually the ones that manage to raise sizeable funds. That is happening in India, too. As the majority falls by the wayside, stories of alcoholism and depression abound. Broken relationships with friends or romantic partners, who were also co-founders, are common.

Then there is the ever-evolving regulation. One man went to jail for no fault of his. And a young boy saw the lives and careers of three entrepreneurs disintegrate right before his eyes. Yet he went on to become an entrepreneur—a very successful one.

~

CHAPTER 1

By the end of the third day it had dawned on Avnish Bajaj that India was a fucked up country.

He had been quite cool when the ordeal began. He was in Delhi and a policeman had come calling. He looked like the quintessential Delhi policeman: the belly and beret were not perfect, and the speech was earthy. Actually, he could have been a policeman anywhere in India.

'*Saab* has asked for you. He wants to do a joint press conference with you.'

This was late in the afternoon of 17 December 2004, a Friday. Avnish was one of the founders of baazee.com, an online auction site and marketplace. He had sold it six months ago to eBay, the United States-based online marketplace, but continued to run it as the country manager.

Not bad, Avnish thought. Finally, he was going to get some recognition for all the hard work his team had done to help the police arrest the young IIT Kharagpur student who had put up video CDs for sale showing teen porn on Baazee one weekend, the previous month.

This CD showed a boy, seventeen, and a girl, sixteen, engaged in oral sex. Both were students of Delhi Public School, Mathura Road. Apparently, the boy had recorded the act and circulated it on mobile phones. The two-minute, thirty-seven-second clip was burned on to video CDs, which were put up on Baazee for Rs 125 apiece.

Baazee's checks and balances kicked in, and the CD was taken off within thirty-six hours, before the weekend ended. But a random Google search could still throw it up because of the layers of indexing and cache.

A journalist googled it. It showed up as a listing on Baazee. A tabloid ran a big story. The Delhi police took suo motu action and filed an FIR.

At the time Avnish was innocent enough not to know that if the police call you on a Friday afternoon, it is nothing but ominous. The office of the economic offences wing to which he was being taken could never be the venue of a press conference. Less naive Indians, when they get such invitations, leave for Dubai. Avnish did call his lawyer, who said it was fine to go.

Sure enough, upon his arrival at the office he was put under arrest. The cyber laws, or whatever semblance of it existed back then, said the CEO of the website was liable. It did not matter who put the offending video CD on it.

No matter, Avnish thought. Slim and dapper, he remained his suave self, laughing and joking with the policemen. There was much mirth when his wife Tina Kapur arrived and signed her name in the register. 'She has a different surname,' one of the cops had observed. 'Are you really married?'

They were, said Avnish, and that Tina was to change her surname at the end of the probation. 'That is not going to happen, now that I have been arrested.'

Amid guffaws, one of the policemen said they had never met someone who was so jovial in custody.

'But I have not done anything wrong. Why worry?' thought Avnish. 'I am in a new industry and these things happen. Surely, they will understand the logic of it.'

Baazee.com was an open marketplace. Anybody could attempt to sell almost anything on it. What's more, Avnish and his team had worked hard through the weekend to identify the fellow who had put up the porn clip, and had him arrested. Avnish really deserved that joint press conference, not the arrest.

The next day, they shifted him to Tihar. And everything changed. The place was freaking scary. 'I am completely innocent and I have been put here in this awful place. Who pays for this?' he had demanded of his lawyer.

'Welcome to India,' said the lawyer. 'This is the system, deal with it.' He is no longer Avnish's lawyer.

Soon, Avnish was talking to the United States Embassy in New Delhi. He was lucky that he was a US citizen, a fact that no doubt escaped the Delhi police.

The Americans intervened through the diplomatic channel. They also tried to educate the Indian authorities about how the cyber laws worked in other countries. With the case now being reported in the global media, the Indian government and authorities became supportive. Soon it looked like the police were nuts, probably trying to divert public attention from other issues.

Avnish got bail after three days—three gruelling, soul-sapping days. But it would be eight years before he got out of it completely. The case went right up to the Supreme Court, whose three-judge bench quashed the whole thing. The cyber laws had been rectified, but that did not help Avnish, because the applicable law is the one prevailing at the time. Thankfully, the Supreme Court concluded that the law was not intended to be interpreted in the way it had been for him.

The experience was extremely traumatic. Today, though, Avnish thinks of it as one of the things that shaped him, made him man up. 'In some ways I am proud of it. If you go to jail for doing something wrong, it is one thing. But you feel like a martyr when you go to jail for an industry.'

The case did shape regulation. The concept of an online marketplace was better understood after that.

~

Kunal Bahl believes that not getting into an IIT was the biggest blessing of his life. He did give the JEE a good shot. But it was not entirely his decision. His parents just assumed that he would take the JEE and follow in his older brother, Nikhil's footsteps. Nikhil had joined IIT Delhi and told everyone his brother would be coming next year.

It was the first time Kunal let someone else make a decision for him, and maybe the last. Things just don't work out when someone else decides for him.

After the failed attempt at JEE, in 2001, Kunal went to work in a manufacturing company for a year. It was his dad's friend's company. He did basic stuff there, like scraping plastic off things, for eight to ten hours a day. He was eighteen, and made Rs 6550 a month. At 4 p.m. every day, he would sit around with the other workers and have tea with them.

It helped open up his mind to other things. The IIT-JEE preparation had made him sick of academics. It had also taught him not to do something if his heart was not in it. The truth is, he wanted to study commerce after class ten. Commerce interested him. Negotiating deals came naturally to him even as a child—small things, like getting his bicycle fixed. But his parents told him there was no future in studying commerce.

His dad worked in the coal mines in Chhattisgarh. He actually worked in the mines, not in a manager's office managing people who did the digging. Financially, it was not very fulfilling.

In 1987–88, when Kunal was about five, his father realized that unless he did something with his career, his kids were not going to get anywhere. So he started a company to make plastic spools around which industrial wires were wound. Later he got into automobile components.

Growing up, Kunal and his older brother Nikhil did not see their father for days on end. He would often leave before the boys woke up and come back after they had slept. Every morning he would drive his Fiat from Greater Kailash, in New Delhi, where they lived, to the factory in Ghaziabad, at a time when there was tonnes of traffic and no flyovers.

The memory of those days has stayed with Kunal as lessons from an entrepreneur's life. An entrepreneur is insanely busy, with little time for family or oneself. But that did not deter Kunal's own aspirations. On the contrary, his father's experience paved the way for Kunal's journey as an entrepreneur. When he decided to set up something of his own, no one in the family questioned it. It was okay to not run after a secure job.

~

As part of the preparations for his engineering entrance tests, Vijay Shekhar Sharma taught himself to read two books at a time, one in Hindi and the other in English, both on the same subject.

He had gone to school in Harduaganj, a small town near Aligarh, in Uttar Pradesh, where his father was a schoolteacher and mother, a housewife. They lived a normal life, under abnormal financial constraints.

His mother told him to prepare well for the engineering entrance tests, for they did not have enough money to send him to a private engineering college.

Vijay had finished class twelve at age fourteen. The teachers at his Harduaganj school had found him too bright for his class more than once, and had made him skip grades, pushing him into the higher levels. But no engineering college would take him before he turned fifteen. That meant for the next one year he had nothing to do but prepare for the JEE.

His schooling had been in the Hindi medium. The engineering tests could be taken in Hindi, but Vijay decided to take them in English, perhaps because the medium of instruction at engineering colleges was to be English.

With time on his hands, Vijay devised a way to study two books simultaneously, both on the same subject, one in Hindi and the other in English. If he had to study, say, physics, he would read the thing first in Hindi and then in English. So if he came across the term 'momentum' in the English book, he would immediately look it up in the Hindi one, finding it there as 'samveg', and move on. That was how he learned his subjects in English.

But not quite well enough. In the entrance tests, which had objective-type questions, he had to first read the multiple answers to fully understand the question. If he saw 'kmph' in one of the answers, he knew the question was about speed.

He understood the questions well enough to make it to the electronics and communications course at the Delhi College of Engineering in 1994. He was not yet sixteen, and required special permission from the university, which was granted as he had ranked high in the tests. Vijay became the youngest student of his batch. And a complete misfit.

'I was cast out by people who were super smart, the cool guys from Delhi. I could barely talk to people, let alone make friends. I was really young, and being so young in a hostel doubled the pressure on me. I would sit in the computer centre, or in the library, and wonder why this notebook computer was called a notebook because it was not a notebook,' says Vijay.

Those traumatic days have become happy memories, now that One97 Communications, Vijay's company, has become one of the most valued start-ups, with a robust business in mobile wallets, an online marketplace under the Paytm brand, and a licence obtained from the Reserve Bank of India to set up a payments bank.

Paytm's office in Noida's Sector 5 is functional, with lots of space, lots of people, and a large reception area teeming with job applicants. Vijay's desk is just a desk, not a cabin, nor in the corner. It is one in a long line of identical desks. On his left, about 25 feet away is a wall with large letters that say: 'We don't need no thought control.' Vijay sits with his back to a busy passage and a row of conference rooms made of glass. We sit in one of those, with a cup of coffee for me that tastes as though it was made in a Noida dhaba, and a sandwich for him.

Vijay, born in 1978, is great fun to talk to—warm, candid, and sincere. He is slightly thick around the middle and has a high-pitched laugh that frequently punctuates the conversation, more so when talking about his early days.

'Eventually I made some friends at the DCE in whom I could confide and to whom I could confess my lack of worldly knowledge. They told me the notebook computer was called a notebook because it was in the shape of a notebook.'

Vijay learned other words. But he could not shake off the feeling that everyone else around him was just so superior. They were like rock stars. Vijay, on the other hand, had moved from being a topper at his school at Harduaganj to a backbencher at the DCE because he could not understand the questions the professors asked. That made him want to hide in his own shadow. It also made him believe that he had little chance of getting a job, and that he had to do something about it, ideally something other than seeking a job.

He began to read the newspapers, writing down every word he did not understand and looked up their meaning. Once he began to understand what the newspapers printed, he moved on to magazines. He started going to the second-hand books market that spreads itself out every Sunday morning on the pavements of Daryaganj and Asaf Ali Road. There he picked up copies of *Fortune* magazine.

~

One evening in 1998, there was not enough air left to breathe in an apartment in Besant Nagar on Chennai's MG Road. At least thirty policemen had come calling, led by someone whose uniform said he was a much bigger officer than an inspector, probably a superintendent of police (SP).

Not all of them could enter the apartment, though. It was small—800 square feet, at most. There was a central hall as you entered. A small room to the left of the hall, which could take in no more than three persons at a time, and another, somewhat larger room on the other side. And there was a tiny dining room, next to the kitchen.

The apartment was shared by three entrepreneurs. In the central hall sat Mohan. Hari worked in the small room on the left. Sri Vatsan was given the larger room, because he had a couple of computers.

Yogendra Vasupal was barely eighteen then, a student of class twelve. He was in that house because he was working as an intern to all the three guys who had their offices in it. Yogi was a brave boy. He had won a few bets from his friends by going to the burial ground in Besant Nagar and spending an hour there in the dead of the night after a drinking session.

But the evening the police came, Yogi was scared, mostly because he could not understand why they were there. They had no business being there. Nothing wrong could possibly transpire in that tiny apartment.

Vatsan ran an online train ticket booking company. Hari used to buy web space in bulk—at that time, 3 GB was bulk—

and went around convincing owners of drug and grocery stores to buy some of that space—say 2 MB—to park their web page so they could be found by Internet users. Mohan was a cameraperson who dreamed of shooting movies some day.

Yogi had a great time there. He would go on sales rounds with Hari, learning a lot from the way Hari made a pitch and the way he spoke to his prospective clients. He learned about the Internet from Vatsan, who was thirty-eight, had no children, and treated Yogi like a son.

The first six months were great. Vatsan's ticketing business was doing well. IRCTC was not yet online. So ticket buyers would place an order for tickets with his company over the telephone or through email, and pay cash on delivery. Two of Vatsan's boys would stand in the queue for tickets. And someone, at times Yogi, would deliver them.

The police came for Vatsan. He was not registered as a travel agent with IRCTC. The reservation counter fellow had noticed the same two or three boys frequently booking large numbers of tickets. He had complained.

Vatsan did not show up for the next two months. Even his wife did not know where he was. Finally, she and Yogi engaged a lawyer, who found out that Vatsan was in Chennai central jail.

He was a broken man when he came out. After that, every time Yogi stayed over at his place, Vatsan cried. A budding technology entrepreneur, who had 512 kbps of Internet speed in 1998, had been destroyed. The last time Yogi saw him was years ago, at a tea shop, wearing a torn T-shirt. A far cry from the elaborately dressed gentleman Yogi remembered.

Meantime, Hari married and began to feel the pressures of a family man. He had invested a lot of money in buying web space but was not able to sell much of it. He started to complain of frequent headaches, for which he would take an Avil. Soon he switched to spasmopoloxin, which women took for cramps during their periods. It gave Hari a high, but as his addiction continued, the medicine gradually reduced the clear-thinking, smart man that Yogi remembered, to a slothful, dull fellow.

Mohan, the aspiring cinematographer, never got a break. He shut shop. Yogi does not know where he is or what he is doing, but he knows Mohan is no longer pursuing his dreams.

The young Yogi watched on as three entrepreneurs failed right before his eyes, one crushed by the environment, the other by stress, and the third because he just gave up. Yet, instead of being disheartened, Yogi went on to become an entrepreneur himself and set up Stayzilla, India's largest online marketplace for 'stays'. When you go to its home page, you cannot miss the chat window that promises you all the assistance you need. It is a unique facility that traces its roots to Vatsan's ticketing chat service. And the way Yogi talks and makes pitches has a clear imprint of Hari's flair.

There is one more thing Yogi learned from his experience in Besant Nagar, Chennai: 'You can get fucked in India for any reason. You have to be tough.'

The lessons of those three entrepreneurs came back to him a few years ago when he realized he was knocking back a bottle of scotch in two days—all by himself.

~

On the evening of 2 August 2011, a Tuesday, Sandeep Aggarwal received a phone call at his Fremont, California home from the big, well-known venture capital fund that had promised to invest $5 million in his start-up, ShopClues, which he was setting up with wife, Radhika Ghai Aggarwal and two friends, Sanjay Sethi and Mrinal Chatterjee.

The phone call was short. But that would take nothing away from the turmoil it was about to cause.

'Sorry, we can't,' said the fellow on the line, or something like that. 'Typically it does not really happen . . . but . . . we think Amazon is going to enter India. Unfortunately we will not be able to go ahead with it.'

It was kind of late in the day for the VC firm to change its mind. On the basis of the VC's promise, Sandeep had quit Caris & Company, where he was managing director and senior Internet analyst. Radhika had shut down FashionClues, her reasonably popular blog. Sanjay had resigned as senior director, products, at eBay, and would leave the company in August. Mrinal had started the process to leave Contenix Inc. by September.

Containers were lined up outside the homes of Sandeep and Radhika, Sanjay and Mrinal. The stuff they wanted to ship to India was being loaded. The three families were moving to Gurgaon, where ShopClues was to be based. The children had been pulled out of their schools. Their school admissions in Gurgaon had been worked out. Radhika had flown in to do a round of the schools, and when she returned, Sanjay flew in to meet the principals. He made video recordings of the school campus and its activities for his partners back in Fremont.

It was a big shift. All of them had spent most of their adult life in the United States. Radhika still thinks of California as home in some way. They have friends there, a social circle. She had known her drycleaner for a while. Her hairdresser knew exactly what to do. Her older son's nanny, a lovely Mexican girl, had stayed on for the younger one.

Moving to India was a considered decision. It was the right place to do consumer Internet. Tickets had been booked. The office in Gurgaon was almost finalized.

Radhika rang Sanjay, who took the call in the middle of his farewell speech to eBay colleagues at the Elephant Bar in San Jose. The rest of his speech passed quickly. He was soon over at Sandeep and Radhika's house with wife, Nupur. Mrinal was tied up elsewhere and could not join them.

Nupur and Radhika were close friends (Radhika calls her Kitty). The ladies went out and bought alcohol and ice cream. Sanjay, Radhika and Nupur sat up all night and talked about their options and what to do next, whether they should go back to their jobs. Not Sandeep, though. Sometime in the middle of the night, he had stood up, put his hands up, and said: 'We will see what to do in the morning.'

Always an early riser, always full of energy, he had already been making calls by the time the other three woke up. They soon joined him in making calls. By Thursday night, they had already spoken to a number of family, friends and people they had worked with, people who had known them for a while. Many of them wrote cheques and said, here you go. Just like that. In less than forty-eight hours since the VC had called, they raised $1.8 million from a dozen angels. One of them was venture capitalist Siddharth Talwar of Lightbox. The others will remain unknown for some more time.

They caught he flights they were booked on. The containers were shipped.

'He is fascinating,' says Radhika of her husband.

It is apparent she is still in love with him.

'Yeah, I am,' her voice rises to a high pitch.

They met at college in Indore, when Radhika was nineteen and Sandeep a couple of years her senior. He likes to say he has known Radhika longer than her parents have.

Radhika met me at the ShopClues office in Gurgaon—a bustling, highly functional place full of little conference rooms on the ground floor, all glass walls and glass doors. She takes me to a larger, quieter, posher one on the first floor.

She is tall, slightly stooping, and certainly not the effervescent, fresh-faced entrepreneur that dots the start-up scene. She is past forty. 'Sad about that,' she says, in the high-pitched falsetto her voice takes from time to time. She has the look of someone who has been around the block. But there is a tremendous change in her demeanour when she smiles and talks in her crisp voice, with just a hint of an American accent. She suddenly appears much younger—interested and animated.

It fascinates her that I use two recorders, one a Blackberry phone I was using at the time and the other a PlayBook, the Blackberry tablet that very few in the world have bought.

'It is a Blackberry tablet!' she exclaims at the second one, as I sip at the sweetest coffee I have had in a while. 'We sold some at end-of-life at one-third the price. Good products, but a brand that just died.'

Yep, BBM was quite something.

'They just did not move away from the business positioning. They should have gone into consumer and people who were using it non-business wise.'

Maybe Apple could have still killed the Blackberry?

'But there was an option to evolve in life. That is a mistake many of us make. We think we are set, but we are not. If you are already set in a profession, you lose the appetite for risk and that is the end of any entrepreneurial ambition you might have.'

However, growing up, there was one risk that Rdhika was determined not to take. She won't marry an army officer and move from place to place the way she had done with her father.

~

By the time Suchi Mukherjee finished speaking, her managing director had tears in his eyes. Suchi had spoken about why she was at Lehman Brothers and not anywhere else. She had been with the investment bank for two years, plucked out of campus at the London School of Economics. But it had been much longer since the last time she had spoken on stage. That was back in school.

Her father believed that all great leaders needed to be great orators. He also believed that both his daughters would one day be leaders. At least he tried everything he could to equip them for it.

Both of Suchi's parents had come from Bangladesh. Her mother, Anjali, from Faridpur, and father, Kalipada, from Barisal. Kalipada's uncle lived in Faridpur. From the time they were very young, Kalipada would meet Anjali every time he visited his uncle in Faridpur.

Both families moved to India at the time of the Partition. Kalipada was the kind of guy who, given a chance, would stay locked in a room and read all day. He came from a modest background but rose in life by doing well in his studies. He spent a long time working with the Industrial Finance Corporation of India, and at one time, sat on the boards of well-known companies.

Anjali, on the other hand, came from a massive zamindar family of Faridpur. Their mango groves stretched as far as the eye could see. They lost everything during the Partition and had to start life afresh in Kolkata.

When Anjali's father passed away, the family discovered that all their property papers were lost. Anjali's mother and her six daughters and four sons went days without food. Anjali was the oldest of six daughters, and very good at mathematics. But she studied humanities because it was cheaper. The next twenty years were terrible for the family, but Anjali stood like a rock to support them. She did not marry until each of her younger sisters was a graduate, at a time when girls were not encouraged to study for too long. All her traditional Brahmin relatives told her she was being a fool. That if she did not marry in her twenties, she would never find a husband. But she did, in her mid-thirties. She married Kalipada in 1970.

He had waited for Anjali.

Kalipada also taught their daughter, Suchi, to drive when she was thirteen. Of course, she was underage. And her mother was furious.

'It is a perfectly sane rule that prevents children from driving,' she said. 'Why break it?'

But the father was unfazed. He wanted Suchi to know that age did not come in the way of anything. He wanted her to do something that was way beyond her years. Something that would show her that nothing was too big for her.

He mandated that everyone had dinner together at 9 p.m. At the dining table he replayed some of what happened at his office that day. He would present conflict situations to his daughters and ask them to come up with solutions.

When Suchi finished class ten at Gyan Bharti, Saket, in New Delhi, she got into Delhi Public School, R.K. Puram. The day of her admission her father said: 'I am not coming with you. Do it on your own. I will come only if you say you cannot do it without your parents.'

Of course, Suchi would say no such thing. She was perhaps the only student that day who handled her admission formalities without a parent by her side.

There was one thing, though, that made Suchi accept defeat: public speaking. From an early age her father had pushed her into it. So much so, some of her earliest memories are of going up on a stage and starting to cry. One day, after yet another tearful appearance and exit, the father, who was, as always, in the audience, said they should stop with it. He was firm, but his eyes may have been moist.

Suchi continued to do well in academics. She had an unusual routine as a student. She would wake up at 3.30 a.m.

every morning, study for two hours, then go to sleep—to wake up again just before it was time to leave for school.

It worked for her. She had jaundice three months before her class twelve final exams, but still managed to score enough to get admission into the St. Stephen's economics honours course. From there she got a scholarship to study economics at Cambridge in 1994. Then followed yet another scholarship to the London School of Economics.

But Suchi was not sure. She wrote to her professor at St. Stephen's, saying she wanted to be an academic. India needed change and she would like to be an agent of it, by teaching. The professor wrote back: 'Put your admission on hold. Come back. Have a taste of what it is like to be an academic in India.'

In 1996, at age twenty-two, Suchi became the youngest to teach economics at St. Stephen's. For a year, she taught development economics to third years. She would go to the college at 8.40 a.m. in the morning and teach. Later, she would go to ICRA, the credit rating agency, where she had found herself a part-time job because her professor wanted her to get a taste of the financial world too.

By the end of the year, she had decided to go back to the London School of Economics and study finance.

It had soon become clear to her that no one in her class wanted to study. It was exactly how it was when she was in college herself. 'I don't know why I forgot that,' she said, when we met.

We met twice, both times in the early morning at the Delhi Golf Club, right after her gym session. The first time was in mid-January, in the particularly severe winter of 2015. But even in that biting cold, not once did her speech falter. One of the brightest entrepreneurs I have met, Suchi chooses her words with care. For instance, she wouldn't say 'upliftment', she says 'uplift', which is the correct usage.

It was difficult to imagine her freezing on stage at any stage of her life. But what is life without its little curiosities?

The day she finally broke her stage fright barrier at Lehman and made her managing director sentimental, she called her father. 'Baba,' she said, 'I owe it to you.' She is now a favoured speaker at corporate dos. She could not see her father's eyes, but they may have been moist yet again.

~

Dhiraj Rajaram's growing-up years were divided almost equally between Chembur in Mumbai and Chennai's Kilpauk and Anna Nagar. He can speak Chennai Tamil and Mumbai Hindi with equal ease.

He met Ambiga in 1992 when they were both seventeen and had just joined the College of Engineering in Guindy, now known as Anna University. He proposed to her within thirty days of meeting her. She took three-and-a-half years to say yes.

At first she thought he was crazy, someone she would have to deal over time, though, she found herself drawn to this thoughtful fellow who was somehow very different from the other boys.

But she laid several conditions, the first of which was that Dhiraj must get a job before they could plan a future together. A conservative girl from a small town in Tamil Nadu, Ambiga wanted her parents to agree to the match. And she wanted Dhiraj's grades to improve.

'I am a slow learner,' he says. 'Even now, I can't read a lot. I actually listen a lot, watch movies a lot. For me those senses, stimuli . . . audio visual . . . are more engaging. But when I like something, I can't let it go. I become obsessive-compulsive about it. If I had to prepare for an exam and had to learn ten chapters, I might be stuck at the second because I liked it.'

Both managed to get job offers from TCS after completing their course in 1996. Neither took it. Ambiga got a scholarship to study at the University of Maine in the United States, Dhiraj at the Wayne State University in Michigan—both as research assistants.

Before they left for the US, Dhiraj, all of twenty-one, met Ambiga's father to ask for her hand in marriage. 'Her father felt it was perhaps the worst decision she could have made. But, over time, he started liking me in some small ways.' They got married twice, first in the US and then in India, because the marriage in the US—which had Dhiraj's Bangladeshi and Chinese fellow research assistants as witnesses—did not feel real as it consisted of only paperwork. There had been no ceremony.

Ambiga went on to join Motorola's research arm and worked in a number of interesting areas—the initial development of Bluetooth, context-aware computing etc.— and became an inventor. Dhiraj went on to work as a consultant at Pricewaterhouse Coopers before leaving the job to do his MBA in the University of Chicago. The next stop was Booz Allen Hamilton.

He did not take a salary for the first three-and-a-half-years after starting Mu Sigma. The initial days were not easy, but they filled Dhiraj with the belief that one has to pay the price of entrepreneurship to be able to fully value it. As part of that payment, Dhiraj, one fine day, spoke to Ambiga about the need to sell their house in Illinois.

Ambiga is a clear-thinking person. She took about ten minutes to agree.

~

On the third day, Phanindra Sama gave up. He wanted to go back to the real world, exactly as the vipassana instructor had predicted. 'All of you will want to run away by the third day,' the instructor had said.

Considerable thought had gone into his decision to join the ten-day programme where one meditated in silence. But three days into it and Phani was beyond caring.

The day began at four in the morning and ended at nine at night. There were ten hours of meditation during the day with some breaks in between. Everyone attending the course observed a 'noble silence'—silence of body, speech, and mind. One could not communicate with fellow meditators, not even through gesture.

Phani is a man of medium height and build and has a mop of hair covering most of his forehead. As a young lad, he could speak fluent Telugu and Hindi, but learned to speak English only after joining BITS Pilani in 1998. But whatever language he spoke, his conversation was always free-flowing and punctuated by frequent chuckling. At the vipassana, the days and nights of silence got to him. He was only allowed to speak to the instructor, and he decided to use that facility to inform him he was leaving.

The instructor sat Phani down and reminded him why he had come to the vipassana in the first place. That was because Phani had had enough of the real world. His world.

This was in the middle of 2009. For the first time in his four years as an entrepreneur, Phani's mind was racing ahead of him. He could no longer quell the impudent thoughts. Had he make a mistake? Had he screwed his life up?

Phani and I meet at his rented apartment in C.V. Raman Nagar in Bangalore on a Sunday in early January 2015. He has promised me a non-vegetarian lunch. His pretty and soft-spoken wife, Sarika, looks a bit distressed because of her maid's illness. Their daughter, of two years and two months, is prancing from the kitchen to her father's lap and back. Their infant son is sleeping in a room inside. Phani laughs

easily and readily, even while talking about his difficulties
with the English language.

He grew up with his uncle, his mother's brother. His
parents lived in a village in Nizamabad, Telangana, and
wanted Phani to get an English-medium education. They put
him in a boarding school as soon as he entered kindergarten,
but he began to fall ill very often when he was in standard
one. So they pulled him out of the boarding school and got
him to stay with his mama in Nirmal.

When he reached standard seven, his mama got
transferred to Hyderabad, and Phani moved with him. He
did eleventh and twelfth grades in a school in Guntur, and
secured admission into the electronics course at BITS Pilani in
1998. That was where he met Charan and Sudhakar.

This was Phani's first time outside his state, his first feel
of people from all parts of the country. He had gone all alone
to get himself admitted into BITS. His parents could not
accompany him because someone in the extended family had
died. So they sent Phani with a friend and the friend's father.

It was good to meet all those new people, but there was
a problem. Phani could not speak English very well. English
was what tied together all the students at BITS, with their
varied backgrounds. Phani had done his schooling in the
English medium, but English was not the language he spoke
at school. It was either Hindi or Telugu.

During one of the ragging sessions, some of his seniors
from Nizamabad discovered he was from the same area
as them. They bonded and the seniors told Phani to make
himself busy outside the hostel if he wanted to be ragged less.
Join one of the extracurricular departments, they said.

BITS had several of those—dance, music, photography,
and others—that recruited their members in the first two
months of a new batch joining. Phani liked the photography
department; it was the hippest of the lot. It organized an

outstation trip every semester and several other activities as
well. For each, a boy would be paired with a girl. But for some
unexplained reason, the department set great store on fluency
in English (boys who have stammered in front of girls might
understand this). Phani needed a bit of a push from his seniors
to get in.

Once in the department, Phani became friends with half
a dozen others there. They hung around together, attended
classes together, and bunked classes together. Phani scored a
CGPA (cumulative grade points average) of more than nine
in the first semester without spending much time studying
because his schooling was strong. He found that the first two
years at BITS were easy, as the curriculum consisted of what
he had already dealt with in school.

Work got serious in the third year. But Phani could do well
in the exams without working too hard. That left him enough
time to spend elsewhere. He became head of the department
of photography in the third year. He also became a very good
photographer, one who excelled at portraits. During festivals,
members of the department of photography would be all over
the campus. Anyone could hail them to take a picture.

The photos would later be printed and sent to the subjects.
The fee for the photograph would be added to the buyers'
mess bill. There were no phone cameras then, so this was a
brisk business. Every semester, the department would call for
tenders to develop the photos. Bribes were offered to win the
contract.

This is how Phani got his first taste of running a commercial
enterprise. He also began to speak better English, as his gang
corrected him every time he made a mistake.

Most of those who graduated from BITS with good grades,
as Phani did in 2002, would enrol for post-graduation, but
Phani was not interested. 'In retrospect, I think I never liked
doing the regular thing.'

All he wanted to do was to build a microchip.

That was the kind of thing that fascinated him. As a child, he was mesmerized by how, at the mere flick of a switch, the fan would begin to run or the light bulb begin to glow. It enchanted him because he could not understand the cause and effect. It appeared to be magic. The science behind it began to reveal itself only when he learned about electrons from class six onwards.

His curiosity only grew. As a child he somehow managed to acquire a small electronics kit with a soldering gun. He would take apart a toy and put it back together. Or at least try to. He also built a solar cooker. The only problem was that it did not work. From there to electronics engineering was a path easy to predict.

So when ST Micro made him an offer on the BITS campus, Phani jumped at it. Only to regret it every day of the year he spent working at the company.

Phani expected to build real microchips while with ST in Delhi. The French-Italian company, headquartered in Geneva, was a large manufacturer of semiconductors and microchips. Phani had built some chips at BITS, but that was as different from making a real chip as dissecting guinea pigs in a biology laboratory is from performing surgery on a human being.

ST was a great company, but it had its ways. 'It was good, but I was not very successful there. I was not in sync with what was happening.'

The first three months were spent in orientation. The company hired in large numbers, but appeared to be in no great hurry to make them do things. So Phani had little to do at work, and nothing when he went back home from work. He was single, and missed his friends and family. Besides, he longed to do something.

He tried to go to office on weekends, but ST, with an entrenched belief in work-life balance, would not let an employee just walk into office on a weekend. One needed special permission.

Phani envied his friends who had joined Texas Instruments in Bangalore. They were always talking about what they were building. As luck would have it, Texas recruited en masse from ST after Phani had completed a year there. He was one of many who applied and got selected, and moved to Bangalore in 2003.

~

Shashank N.D. did have an appointment with Dr Murli R. of Aesthetics Dental Clinic in Malleswaram, Bangalore, but when he arrived at the clinic, the doctor asked him to wait just a little bit. There were patients queued up and the doctor's schedule was going haywire, as doctors' schedules tend to. There was no harm, Murli thought, in asking Shashank to wait because he was not there to get himself treated but to sell a software.

Except that after a busy day of seven meetings behind him, Shashank could have done with a bit of physical comfort, if not dental care. But he waited in the reception area. As he sat down, he was overcome by exhaustion. It was close to 9 p.m. However hard he tried, he could not keep awake. He fell asleep right there in his chair.

He woke up when he felt somebody shaking him by the shoulder. It was Dr Murli. All the patients had gone, leaving only a sleeping Shashank in the reception area. He woke up with a rash of apologies. But the doctor was sympathetic.

'You know what,' said the doctor, 'I have not seen such an exhausted person in my life. And you know what, just for that I am going to buy your software.' By that yardstick, Shashank should have signed a deal a day. Long days were hardly uncommon for him.

Shashank is now an active member of iSPIRT, Sharad Sharma's organization that supports product entrepreneurship. When Sharma first met Shashank and Abhinav Lal, who had set up Practo, he found both the young founders in a rather feverish state of mind. Shashank had not slept for almost an entire week. He slept very little those days anyway.

This was 2012, and Practo had recently raised money in Series A. It had moved into a small but proper office, from the home office Shashank and Abhinav used to run. And life had become a little more chaotic. The founding pair used to work till they collapsed—when all the fuel of all the Red Bulls they used to consume finally ran out—and rolled off gently into the bed stationed strategically close to their work desk.

By then it would be 5 a.m. Two hours later, they would wake up to get ready for the first meeting of the day. Everything appeared to be in a daze; it was like being on a drug.

Still, they contributed to the iSPIRT fund, at a time when they had very little money. Shashank has no recollection of what Sharad told him. Just that it left him with the overwhelming feeling that this could help build better products and a better India.

That is important to Shashank. He thinks of death as a great leveller. Everyone, however big, will eventually find himself six feet under, at the same level as everyone else. What will matter is what he leaves behind, and whether it is bigger than himself.

To Shashank, it matters what Practo is doing to the healthcare system—which is, giving patients and doctors access to one another, and making medical records easy to store and use. It is not about a couple of people building something. It is about building products that can change the world.

'In 100 years, the world will be a much better place if we all can get our act together. Whatever good you do is going to come back to you in some way. I am a huge believer in karma. You don't worry about what you can get, you worry about what you can give. We wanted to give. We gave what we could. We participated in their events. We have worked with NASSCOM, too.'

Shashank seems to have accumulated a lot of good karma. He and Abhinav set up Practo in 2008, soon after graduating from the National Institute of Technology at Surathkal. Soon, the world changed, as Lehman Brothers fell on 15 September 2008.

To their credit, Shashank and Abhinav managed to raise seed funding of half-a-million dollars in 2010–11 from Sequoia. At that time, nobody was investing in a start-up. It was Sequoia's first seed funding in India. Both Shashank and Abhinav were twenty-three, probably the youngest people in whose venture Sequoia had invested anywhere in the world. It put in another $4 million in 2012, as Series A funding.

Practo is now one of the unicorns, the term used to describe a start-up valued at more than a billion dollars. It is acquiring companies.

Tall and well-dressed, wearing a full-sleeved shirt buttoned at the cuffs and a newly cultivated stubble, thoughtful, measured and articulate, Shashank did not rest his elbows on the table even once during our two-hour lunch at the sylvan, open-air setting of the Oberoi's Thai restaurant in Bangalore. He says he loves Thai food so much he would walk many miles for it.

Shashank no longer uses an alarm to wake up. He has read studies that say an alarm forces your body to wake up, which is not good for it. If you wake up on your own, it means you have completed your sleep cycle. He avoids scheduling meetings before ten in the morning. He does not feel sleepy in the afternoon. And he does not collapse from his work desk into his bed.

At our lunch he drinks sparkling water. There is no sign of Red Bull.

~

CHAPTER 2

The Tihar experience would have rattled anyone from Avnish Bajaj's upper middle class background. His father was in the Directorate General of Mining Safety, a branch of the civil services. His was a transferable job, and Avnish grew up in small towns all over the country—Dhanbad, Asansol, Jabalpur, Shahdol, Ajmer, Hyderabad (the last one not so small). Thankfully for Avnish, all these towns had missionary schools, which gave young Avnish a sense of continuity in his education and environment. In 1986, when he entered class eleven, he was admitted into Delhi Public School, Mathura Road.

Until then, his performance as a student had been a roller coaster; every once in a while he would top the class and every once in a while he would fail in some subjects. His first love was sports, and studies his last. It was only in class ten that he started focusing on studies. He had flunked in physics in the ninth grade and in mathematics in the eighth.

When he entered class ten, one of the older kids he used to play with acquired a high rank in the IIT-JEE, somewhere between 120 and 130. This boy was Avnish's senior at the De Nobili School in Dhanbad. He became an instant celebrity in the officers' colony where Avnish's family lived. The ranker was felicitated at the club. People in the colony talked about him endlessly—what a good boy and worthy son he was.

The fanfare got Avnish interested. The route to fame, he figured, was IIT. That accomplished what scores of people—parents, relatives, the uncles and aunts of the officers' colony—had failed at, despite their having lectured about it till they went blue in the face. Avnish became serious about his studies. The results followed.

Once at DPS, Mathura Road, he pretty much gave up his life for two years. All he did was study for the IIT-JEE. When the results came, Avnish stood at rank twenty-four, the highest in the history of DPS Mathura Road. He could choose any IIT and any stream. He chose computer science at IIT Kanpur.

The first shock of his life awaited him at IIT Kanpur.

Avnish had had a protected childhood. Despite moving often from one town to another, the environment around him was consistent, even if the people inhabiting it changed. There was always an officers' colony, and always a missionary school. IIT Kanpur was far removed from both.

He was now in the midst of students who came from all kinds of backgrounds in terms of language, culture, habits, concerns . . . everything. Secondly, the pressure was intense. You could smell the competition in the air. If you did not excel in academics, you were a nobody. Avnish sought a transfer to IIT Delhi. It was denied.

So he took the only route available to him. He reconciled himself to his fate, settled down, adjusted to and accepted his surroundings, made friends and, after four years, graduated second in his class. And then went to the US.

This was 1992. When you graduated from IIT, you went to the US. That was the done thing, the natural progression.

Avnish went to the University of Wisconsin, in Madison, concealing two big disappointments in his heart. He had really wanted to top his at IIT Kanpur. And now that he had finished second, he did not get the university of his choice, Berkeley.

Today he laughs while talking about this. But that was the kind of pressure the system put on you. It has had an impact on how he thinks about success and his children, which is the exact opposite of what he had felt as a student. He wants his children—a boy of eight and a girl of four —to develop their own potential, instead of going through a rote system.

~

Fortune magazine told Vijay Shekhar Sharma about Silicon Valley in California, the hub of technology start-ups. This was 1995–96. There was magic going on in the valley. There was the Internet, there were Yahoo, Netscape, Marc Andreessen, Jerry Yang. There was a popular belief in the valley that people who did not complete their education created great companies. That gave Vijay hope: if he did not pass college, he could still do something, such as build an Internet company. And, instead of waiting for their final exams, Vijay and a friend started a company while still in college. They named it XS Corps.

XS Corps built content management systems for the web. Vijay had a business card that said: East 37, K Gate, New Delhi. It meant East Hostel, Room No. 37, Kashmiri Gate. It had the DCE computer centre's phone number as the office number and the hostel's number as the residence phone. They aspired to get a pager. But that was expensive. So they made friends with a shopkeeper nearby and used his telephone number as their office number on their business card. When someone called, the friend in the shop would say

Vijay was not in, or away in a meeting, and take down the caller's number. Later Vijay would return the call.

Vijay noticed there were several job advertisements from companies for employees who could work on their content management systems and related technologies. He would go for these interviews and say, 'I'm not here for the job. But I have a company that can do this job for you.'

Some 'interviewers' did not take this kindly. 'Why did you waste my time?' they would ask. Some others would remark: 'Interesting! But how will you do it?'

'We have computers in college. I will do it and send it over email.'

Some money began to come in. However, given his background, Vijay, upon finishing his engineering degree in 1998, felt compelled to get a job. That he did, with a company called RiverRun Software Group in Noida. His position was in business development. He left the job in less than a year and went back to his own company full-time. It was pointless to waste time in a job that did not excite him when he could be running his own company. His parents, because of whom he had taken up a job in the first place, were disappointed; not least because RiverRun would have sent Vijay to the United States.

Vijay cut a deal with his parents. He would continue to send the same amount of money home every month if they allowed him to work in his own company.

One of his first clients was Living Media India, which published a host of magazines, such as *India Today* and *Business Today,* and would go on to make it big in news television with *Aaj Tak*. XS Corps built LMI's search platform, a couple of websites, their back-end systems, and provided them with the required Internet technology.

In 1999, XS Corps got an offer it could not refuse from Lotus Interwork, based in New Jersey. Vijay, the chief founder of XS, and three of his co-founders shared equally the Rs 1 crore they received from Lotus. That was a lot of money in those days, and Vijay started to live a king's life in Noida, now as a Lotus Interwork employee.

One evening he was out at dinner with friends at Punjabi by Nature in Noida's Sector 18, a sort of expensive place. His friends ordered golgappa shots with vodka. Vijay, who does not drink alcohol, told the waiter to serve him golgappas without the vodka. But he was charged the same rate as the vodka shot golgappas. He did not quite care about this though. The money from the sale of XS was in the bank and a fat salary was coming every month, now that he worked for a US MNC. There were also reimbursements.

But Vijay was not happy. It irked him that he was only doing the India development work for an American company. Around him, the Internet was spreading its tentacles. Dotcoms were burgeoning. The euphoria around indya.com, jaldi.com, contest2win, IndiaGames, and others was probably more heady than that it is around the Flipkarts and Snapdeals of today.

In the meantime, Lotus wanted Vijay to go to the US. At the visa interview, he was asked for his bank statement, which he had not carried with him. He was asked to come again. But he did not go. Instead, he quit to follow his heart, which was in building his own company.

In quick succession, Vijay started three companies. The first was an Internet service provider, Chemistry Online. 'The damn thing did not work because the last mile connectivity sucked.'

The second was a people search Internet company called White Pages. 'That did not work because there was no money you could make on white pages in India.'

The third was One97, a telecom services company, which started operations by giving mobile users contact information about people on SMS, similar to White Pages. It started in December 2000, with mixed initial results, until an eye-opener of an idea that came from I.B. Saxena of bababazar.com, who knew Vijay.

'You have this people search data, why don't you give it to me on sms?' Saxena said.

Vijay had no problems with that. He did not even ask what was in it for him. But one day Saxena sent him a cheque from a mobile operator who had made money by using Vijay's data. Interestingly, Vijay was not making any money on the Internet, which was the original idea, but had now made some through this offline route.

Let's go and do something more with the mobile operator, thought Vijay, and hit upon the revenue sharing model. The operator would charge its consumers for the data taken from Vijay, and the two would split the money the consumer paid. Gradually, mobile operators started taking from Vijay content other than people search data. The breakthrough came when Airtel wanted astrology content, on voice.

'I had a panditji sitting in office, attending calls and answering questions on the computer,' says Vijay, and laughs his high-pitched laugh of delight.

The astrology content on voice grew ten-fold for Airtel, more money came in, but Vijay was not satisfied. 'I was a technology guy; I could analyse call traffic data, and wanted to do more: music, cricket—that sort of thing.' Thus, way back in 2001–02, One97 started providing cricket scores on a dial-in number, as well as music. It acquired one of the first licences to play music on the phone in this country, and that started bringing in some money.

Airtel had recently acquired JT Mobile's mobile licence for Punjab. The circle head for that region wanted music content on a fifty-fifty revenue share. Not surprisingly, given the love for music in Punjab, the service grew rapidly. One97's relationship with Airtel expanded to other circles.

One97 grew bigger. And got into bigger problems.

~

Radhika Ghai had studied in many schools in so many cities, she has lost count of them—between eight or ten. Her dad was in the army. They lived in army colonies. If Radhika's family was not moving, her friends' were. It was a constant churn. Radhika loved it.

It taught her to adapt to new places, people, friends, teachers and social life. It taught her to fit in. But she was not ready to adapt to life as an army wife. In spite of the blessings of her childhood, that came from moving places, she did not want to do it all her life. She could not avoid the twinge of jealousy she felt towards her cousins who had spent years in the same town and built enduring associations. She, too, wanted to settle down in one place and live there.

She got half her wish. She did not marry an army man, but the man she did marry moved countries within a year of their wedding. And they have moved—here the pitch of her voice rises dramatically again—every two years since then. 'Oh my god! Oh my god, yes! Totally new cultures, but it has been a fun ride.'

Their longest in any place has been in Gurgaon, where they had lived for more than three years at the time Radhika and I met in February 2015.

She studied in convent schools till class six, and then in Kendriya Vidyalayas, where she learned Sanskrit. She also read abridged versions of the Ramayana and the Mahabharata, which were compulsory reading in KV. She finds both to be fascinating stories that get replicated in our lives.

Going to a temple is more a spiritual experience for her than religious. She is fine not going to one for a long time, but, when she does, she feels an aura of spirituality, mostly from the other people who are there, as they all come looking for peace. She loves Hinduism for its accepting nature, not only of Hindus who do not practise the religion every day, but also of the flaws in its own gods.

'I realize that Hinduism is perfect, though our gods are not. Hinduism allows flaws in its gods. How awesome is that! Look at Krishna. He had god knows how many wives. Ram messed up with his wife. Which other religion tells you that your gods are flawed and that is fine?'

She is equally accepting of her own imperfections as an entrepreneur. She calls herself the accidental entrepreneur. She has never been quite sure. She has two sons, born six years apart. At any time, one looked too old to move to India and the other too young. An imminent bonus would hold her back. Or a resolve to lose fifteen pounds by joining the gym would. Or a house they had just bought.

She calls her husband the real entrepreneur and her driving force. He really wanted to do something on his own.

They got married in 1997, when she was twenty-two, and went to live in Singapore. They came back after a year-and-a-half, and Sandeep went to the US to do his MBA in strategy at the Olin Business School at Washington University in St. Louis. A year later, Radhika joined the same business school to study the same course.

Sandeep went on to hold a string of jobs as financial consultant, and became a well-known Wall Street analyst tracking the media and Internet. Radhika joined Goldman Sachs and was working there when the two hijacked planes flew into the World Trade Center on 11 September 2001.

Everything went dark and gloomy. The market tanked. Companies started shutting down. And Radhika realized she was not quite cut out for the suit-and-tie work that Goldman demanded of her.

That was when a friend of hers from St. Louis called. They had done a project together back at school. Now she called to say there was a role open at Nordstrom, the American fashion retailer, where she was working. Radhika took it gladly and moved from New York to Seattle.

She left Nordstrom in 2007. It was not easy. She loved fashion, and the job got her a 40 per cent discount for friends and family. There were other reasons, too, to love the job. It taught her a culture she values and carries with her wherever she goes.

Most organizations put the CEO on top, with vice-presidents and other senior managers below her, and the customer right at the bottom. Nordstrom inverted this structure. The customer was on top, the sales people were right below her, and under the salespeople were the corporate managers to support the sales team. The CEO was right at the bottom, supporting the entire structure.

Once a year, Radhika—like everyone else in the company, regardless of their rank—would go down to the floor in the store and sell something. Her favourite was the women's shoes department. She would help customers try on shoes and fetch the right size for them. It made her feel close to the customer.

She admired the family behind Nordstrom for building it to be the large organization it was. It inspired her. So did the Silicon Valley folklore, with its stories of people creating consistently and beautifully, and husbands and wives teaming up well. Cisco was started by the husband-wife team of Len Bosack and Sandy Lerner. Flickr was started by the husband-wife team of Stewart Butterfield and Caterina Fake. The husband-wife team of Sandeep and Radhika could also pull it off!

Sandeep always wanted to do it. Radhika slowly bought into the idea. The irony is that she became an entrepreneur before he did because she had the flexibility. 'Being a woman has some advantages. If you have a supporting husband, there are many things you can do.'

She started FashionClues, a blog giving fashion advice to South Asian women. It later became a website, with all kinds of content including Bollywood, and a bit of e-commerce. Radhika hired two persons to work with her. The three did everything there was to do.

~

In 1997, within three months of studying finance at the London School of Economics, Suchi Mukherjee got placed with Lehman Brothers in London, the nerve centre of global finance. But there was a problem.

Suchi wanted to come back to India. She had put in her CV with Lehman, which had come to the campus for recruitment, because she wanted to see if she had a proper chance. If she was called for an interview, it would be proof her CV was sound.

When she got the call, she thought she should appear for the interview for practice. That would prep her for the interview for some other job she really coveted.

Lehman put her through ten rounds of interviews. She cleared all ten.

Her masters' class at LSE had more than 100 students. It was a microcosm of the world, quite unlike stodgy Cambridge. She was the first from the class to get placed. But she went to meet a Lehman managing director with her mind made up. She was going to turn the offer down.

'I am going back to India,' Suchi told the managing director.

He was patient, and reasonable. 'I suppose you want to do finance, be it in England or India?'

She said she did.

'If you want to do finance, you have to learn with the best. The big centres are London and New York. We are among the top five investment banks in the world. If not us, who?'

'*Iski baat mein dum hai,*' she thought. (This man is talking sense.)

She took the Lehman job, and did so well the first two years she was one of two to head recruitment across Europe. It was big shit. You got to travel across Europe for three to six months, with an American Express card that had been set no limits, going from college to college, interviewing kids, and wining and dining the ones you liked to make them join Lehman.

She hired one of the biggest ever classes at Lehman, of eighty people. That was Lehman's prime, a peak for NASDAQ, the first Internet boom. Until one morning in the year 2000, when it all began to collapse.

From then on, for the next three years, every day was a nightmare. Lehman shrank. People got fired in the most ruthless ways. Suddenly, one day, their access card would stop working. From a limitless Amex card, they plunged into a situation where the accounts department wouldn't reimburse a bottle of milk if someone put it on their expense account. All of Suchi's work-friends lost their jobs.

She had joined the technology team in 2003. It had twenty-four bankers, which was a decent size. At the end of the year four were left. Suchi was one of them. Everybody else had been fired. Finally, Suchi left Lehman in 2003.

She looks back fondly at her time there because of the good work she got to do, especially in the first two years. Lehman taught her attention to detail. When you started with it at the bottom of the rung, you were like a mini-slave. The bosses were trained to spot the extra gap between a dot and a capital letter. And numbers were sacrosanct.

Suchi was part of a three-member team that created the world's largest aviation insurance company through a transatlantic merger. It gave her the opportunity to audit people's jets and see how badly they spent their money.

She worked on a project to restructure the East European telecom giant, Orange's assets, for which she had to cross the Vienna-Bratislava border in a car at midnight. Bratislava did not have an airport at the time. The border security, using a flash light, peered into her passport and tried to figure out where India was.

Over lunch the next day in Bratislava, Suchi told her senior director working on the deal that she was going to get married. He was horrified. 'You can't get married,' he fumbled. 'First, you are too young, secondly you are in banking. Third I can't let you go to India. Send someone else.'

This was not a deal, Suchi told him. This was a wedding. Her own wedding.

'I said, Andrew, this is not a deal, this is *shaadi*.'

'So send someone else,' the senior director persisted. 'Marry by proxy. You did date by proxy.'

~

We are in Dhiraj Rajaram's large office, the largest of any of the start-up offices I visited for this book. The office, on the fourteenth floor of ITPB in Whitefield, Bangalore, has portraits of Steve Jobs, Bill Gates and Jeff Bezos hung on the walls. To Dhiraj they represent art, science and scale, respectively. There is also a hard-to-miss Nataraj.

Two of the walls are more or less just glass windows that overlook two small ponds. In the near corner from his desk hangs a formal jacket next to a leather one. The leather jacket is for when Dhiraj rides his Bullet motorcycle to work, which he does often.

There is a cricket ball on his desk. It is shiny and clearly unused. But there was a time when Dhiraj played cricket regularly. A left-arm bowler and a right-hand batsman, he played the under-sixteen for the Tamil Nadu Cricket Association. With time, though, cricket left his life.

He is smooth-shaven today, but you can see him with a stubble in some photographs. He has calm eyes that sparkle every once in a while with surprising impishness. 'If you write something Ambiga does not like, I'll have to come and marry you,' he says, and dissolves into laughter. He may not have much margin of error left because he confesses to not being the perfect husband. 'Ambiga has been able to live with me, which cannot be easy. I am very fortunate. All the things that good husbands do, I don't do. Except cooking. That too because I like to cook. I don't celebrate anniversaries and birthdays. It does not even occur to me to.' Ambiga is not just his wife, she is chief operating officer at Mu Sigma.

Which year did they get married?

'Er . . . ninety-eight, I think,' he says, again dissolving into laughter.

Dhiraj quickly shifts from being impish to deeply thoughtful and philosophical. He never consciously wanted to be an entrepreneur. No real entrepreneur consciously wants to become one or decides to be one. That conscious decision is for the 'arranged marriage entrepreneur'—the kind that goes around looking for an idea after having decided to become an entrepreneur.

Dhiraj is a 'love marriage entrepreneur'. His kind falls in love with an idea, hopelessly, helplessly, obsessively. They want to spend their life with the idea. They want to marry the idea just so that the world considers their relationship legitimate.

To the love marriage entrepreneur, the idea of what he is doing is more important than the idea of starting his own company, making money or earning fame.

The idea of Mu Sigma came to Dhiraj. He did not seek it. What he saw while working at Booz Allen was that change was gathering momentum and most people had a very unsporting attitude towards it. At best, they did not want to be affected by it in a negative way. Nobody wanted to benefit from it. Nobody was looking to thrive on it.

'If you want to benefit from change you have to be someone who enjoys change. The word that usually comes to us after change is management. Risk management. Uncertainty management. We don't say change enjoyment. We don't use words like that after change. Why? Why do people feel that way? What are the things that lead to this feeling?' he asked himself. The answer took its time to come.

All of us are a little bit insecure in life, which is understandable. We all love ourselves and that's not a bad thing. What that means is that self-preservation is built into us.

Given that self-preservation is built into us, you can go two ways. If you are valued for something, either you can destroy that something yourself with something new that you seek and if you cannot do so, the only other natural choice you have is to make sure that the value of what you have remains perpetually high. One way to do so is by creating enough moats around that knowledge.

Dhiraj noticed this over and over again in organizations. Those who were experts in an industry were considered sane. Any time a good idea came up, people wanted to protect it, even going to the extent of protecting it through legal or technical means so that nobody else could get their hands on it.

What would happen if the opposite was done? What if, instead of revering knowledge, you showed it a bit of irreverence? Somebody who understands and accepts constant change and believes that the world of constant change is the way things are will tend to be less secretive. He will understand that the small losses that he may have to bear in being less secretive will be far outweighed by the benefits of the number of adjacent possibles that he will see on a constant basis. It is important not just to keep knowledge unlocked, it is also important to realize that old knowledge needs to pave the way for new knowledge.

The destruction of old knowledge will create space for creation. Then you will have learning—constant learning. After all, knowledge broken down is learning and, in Dhiraj's book, is always rated above knowing. 'If you know something and you feel that you know it, that day you stop learning. When you feel you are an expert, you stop experimenting and learning. If you see everything as closed and secretive, you are not using other disciplines.'

Learning over knowing became the dominant perspective. But it had to be attained not with the insouciance of an expert but through the curiosity of a child. It was only curiosity that would lead to extreme experimentation. And the results of the experimentation will not need to be guarded by legal and technical means. They should be free-floating so that ideas collide and intermingle, leading to better and better ideas. The new IP is no longer intellectual property, it is an interdisciplinary perspective. Every discipline is a lens through which we view the world.

Mathematics is a lens, as is physics, as much as biology and history are. The more lenses you can use, the better you see the world. The more you mix and match lenses the more holistically you see the world.

The essence of that can be translated into organizations. That was the new way of thinking Mu Sigma would espouse: make the big companies think like children, like small companies, and be more innovative. If, every time, a small company has to be created and a big one destroyed, a lot of waste would happen in the economy. It would be better if the large companies kept innovating.

'So, I thought, how do you take entrepreneurship into big companies? These big companies are big canvasses. If you can make an impact through those canvasses, you can do much more for the world,' argues Dhiraj.

Clarity emerged from Dhiraj's rumination at Booz Allen as to the why (learning over knowing), the what (extreme experimentation) and the how (interdisciplinary perspective). If the three could be put into practice, they would create an environment and an organization that would benefit from change.

What Dhiraj saw around him was the opposite.

'Companies, once they grew big, invariably became complex. They had capital and talent, but no time. Time was sucked out of them because of the complexity.'

The task at hand was to get the complexity out of these organizations, not by ignoring or dismissing it but by appreciating it and dealing with it. 'Real simplicity is on the other side of complexity,' reflects Dhiraj. 'Take a look at an airplane cockpit, for example. It is a machine designed to take people 30,000 miles up in the air, move them to a destination 3000 miles away and bring them safely back down. You and I might be confused by all the buttons in the cockpit, but for a trained pilot it is the right amount of complexity to achieve the task at hand.'

By now it is difficult to tell whether we are still talking about companies or life philosophies. When did he think of all this?

'The first nine months after starting Mu Sigma. I sat alone. Nobody would listen to me, nobody would talk to me. It was only me. Alone.'

~

Phanindra Sama used to write his CVs from the heart. He did not fill them with the usual clichés (want to work for a professional organization, etc.). In the CV he submitted to Texas, he wrote that he wanted to build a microchip and have it in his pocket in a year.

His entire interview was about this objective. How would he do that? Why was it so important to him? Microchips take years to build, because they have to go through elaborate tests. However, when Phani explained his passion, the interviewer, who had pencilled him in for some other department, put him in the test chip team.

Once in Bangalore, Phani took up a flat near the office, where he lived alone during the weekdays. Weekends would find him in a large flat in Koramangala, which was shared by seven of his friends including Charan and Sudhakar.

However, Phani never really switched off from his chip making. He would put one on simulation, which takes hours, and wake up at all sorts of hours to see if it was working properly. His friends ridiculed him for working so hard even after he had left college, when it was time to have a blast.

Texas was as different from ST as chalk is from cheese. Phani's orientation was instantaneous. The fellow from human resources took him to his manager. The manager said nice to meet you, this is your seat, and this is the circuit we want you to build.

All Phani could say was okay.

A while later, the manager came back to him. 'Can you build it by tomorrow?'

Phani found this exhilarating; this was what he had been looking for. He worked till late that day, his first day on the job, and completed the damn thing.

That became a pattern. Nobody in Texas frowned at someone working till late, or coming to office on weekends. The entire culture cared only about results.

On the long weekends and holidays that Phani did not work and did not have stuff to do with the friends in Koramangala, he would visit his parents in Nizamabad. And since he seldom knew which weekend he might be free, he was always making last-minute travel plans.

Trains were therefore ruled out, since tickets had to be booked days, if not weeks, in advance. So buses it was. Besides, he loved watching the movies they showed on the bus journeys. He would just curl up in his seat and take them in.

Getting tickets was convenient, too, usually from a travel agent.

But things did not work out during the Diwali break of 2005. Phani had put off his decision to go to Nizamabad until the very last moment. Even the travel agent said he did not have any tickets for Nizamabad. All the bus operators he worked with were fully booked. So he called a fellow agent to ask if any of his operators had a seat going empty.

By this time, Phani's mind had begun to whirl. 'Why is this agent calling another agent? He should be able to tell me if any of the operators had seats available.' He tried to brush aside these questions. The important thing was to get a seat and get to his parents. So he went to the other agent, who made a few calls, but still could not get him a seat.

It was a disheartened Phani who came back home, but also one who was constantly thinking about what had just happened. 'Maybe if I had gone to more agents . . . Maybe the agents called the wrong operators . . . If I had approached the operators myself . . . '

These thoughts were still occupying his mind when he woke up the next day, all alone.

'Wait, why can't there be a software where all bus operators could put out the number of buses and seats they had available,' he asked himself. The customer could just log on to the screen, see who had a seat, and call that operator directly.

This would benefit all three—the bus operator, the agent and of course, the customer—because there was a better chance of all tickets getting sold and travellers getting to reach where they wanted to go.

Phani opened his computer and started typing furiously. It was an email to all seven of his mates sharing the Koramangala flat, who had all gone away for the holidays. 'How about creating this software?' he wrote. 'We could invite all BITSians to contribute to the creation of this software. The money it would earn could go to the BITS alumni association.'

Even at this point, the thought of becoming an entrepreneur had not crossed Phani's mind. It was hardly the done thing back then, when few consciously thought along those lines. But he did want to solve the problem that had him holed him up all alone on a festival day.

Sudhakar was the first to write back. 'Let's do it man,' he said. The other six were equally excited.

They prepared a project plan and split the work.

But, wait, weren't these electronics guys? What were they thinking trying to write software?

'None of us knew computer science and web technologies,' admits Phani, with a chuckle. 'We knew C++, which every engineer learns. We did not know Java, .net, HTML, nor web tech, database and server.'

They approached it as a hobby. A fewmonths before Phani's heartbreak at the bus terminus, Charan had written a small software for expense management of the flat in which the seven of them lived. As it happens with a bunch of young men living together, purchases were random. Someone would go out for a stroll and come back with a bagful of tomatoes just because they looked good. Whoever had his wallet the closest to him would end up paying the maid. All these expenses had to be squared off at the end of the month.

The software came in handy. 'Charan was always the creative one, always doing things.'

But the bus ticketing software they were talking about was a little more complex. So the boys went out and bought a bunch of books on how to learn Java, how to write web technology software, and so on. They taught themselves to write software from those books.

Many of their friends told them not to reinvent the wheel. Bangalore was full of software guys. 'Get someone to do it,' they said.

That was wise advice. If bus operators were to rely on this software, it was bound to be complex architecture. If even one thing went wrong, the whole architecture would implode. 'If you are serious about building a product, why learn this entire system?'

But nobody was too serious about it. As in, they really wanted to crack it, but they were also having fun while doing it. And there was no hurry, no time-to-market, no thought of competitors doing it, no pressure.

Gradually, four of the seven mates lost interest. But for the three who remained on the project—Phani, Charan and Sudhakar—it soon grew into a near-obsession. As they learned from the books and started to write the software, it consumed them. This was all they wanted to do after office hours.

Phani was the one to liaise with the bus operators, who were not the gentlest of souls. In fact, they were part of the reason the other four lost heart.

Friends asked Phani what the hell he was doing. 'You are doing well at TI. It is the best paymaster in Bangalore. Will you leave it to get into an industry run by rowdies and *gunda*s? The mafia?' That indeed was the general public impression about the bus industry.

But who was listening? Charan was immersed in the project, just the way he would bury himself in whatever he took up in earnest. He was working for Honeywell then, a large, respected, global company. He used to work on the bus software till very late at night and was often left with little energy to report to office in the morning. So he stopped going to office altogether. Sudhakar was the thoughtful type, weighing out the pros and cons.

The three had known one another a long time. They could shout at one another one minute and talk animatedly the next. More importantly, there was mutual respect. 'That saved us.'

They converted the front room of their first floor house in Koramangala into their office. The landlord lived on the ground floor, and soon got to know that Phani was influencing his tenants to leave their jobs. He told them not to have anything to do with Phani.

They now took up another house in the lane behind the earlier one. Phani left his flat near the Texas office and moved in. All three slept in one bedroom and converted the hall into their office.

They managed to create the software in just six months. 'It takes less time than you think. Things happen magically—not just coding but even running a company. Would you expect a thirty-year-old guy to run a large company like Flipkart? One learns quickly.'

Those were nevertheless a tough six months. Coding was the easy part. The tough part was to figure out how to get inputs from the bus operators for building the software. How did they really work? What kind of software will suit their business? Will they really want a software?

They did not—not initially. 'Many people have tried it,' said an operator. 'People buy airline tickets online, not bus tickets.'

Another one pointed to a customer sitting in his front office and said: 'Look at him, will he ever go online and buy my ticket?'

There was some truth to that. But Phani, Charan and Sudhakar kept going at the software as if their life depended on it, even though it was still a part-time thing for them. Maybe it had, by then, become a challenge to their ego. It would hurt their pride if they could not solve this problem.

Their pursuit was difficult at many levels. These were three guys who had had a good life at the BITS campus, were liked by their teachers, pampered at home, and held good, well-paying jobs where they were valued and respected. Now they were going to bus operators to ask them for a favour—to try out their software. There were operators who would not so much as look at them, but just look through them instead.

'We made fervent requests, we begged, we called them "sir", which is not how we addressed anyone in our offices. My heart would run fast with fear when I had to go and meet with the operators.'

Finally, they got lucky with Rajesh Travels. Its owner had a young son who had also studied engineering and wanted to make a difference. He took them through the varied pace of how things worked for an operator and what he needed. That was a big help in writing the software. But when it was written, it found no takers. Not even Rajesh Travels was interested.

~

Kunal Bahl took his unsuccessful shot at JEE as a sign that he was meant to do something else—just that he was not sure what that something else was.

He wanted to get a good business education. Back then, he was naive and thought they actually taught you something in college. But he did not want to take the usual route of studying engineering, gaining two years of work experience, and then enrolling for an MBA.

He applied to the Wharton School of Business, University of Pennsylvania. It was the only school in the US that gave you an engineering and business degree in five years. Kunal finished it in four to save money.

Those four years felt like a lot more. Kunal did three jobs while doing six to seven courses every semester. He wasn't serving fries though. He did relatively intellectual jobs, like a research or teaching assistantship.

The US system of education inspired him to do a lot of other things—he did courses on writing, on the history of Jewish art, on Western classical music, and on ethnic conflicts around the world.

He also saw a business opportunity in the love for cricket among the Indian students, of whom there were many. The 2003 World Cup was the first to be streamed live online. Kunal bought a full subscription. He used to book a lecture hall every night, where he invited fellow students to watch the matches. Entry was free—Kunal did not want to get into trouble for reselling a consumer subscription—so the halls were more than full every night. But he charged $5 for a samosa and a cola; a lot of which were consumed through the night. The earnings went to CRY America.

In his final year of college, Kunal set up a company, his first, called Dropps. It made detergent, which was sold in Walmart stores. He joined Microsoft after finishing college in 2007. That year there were 120,000 applications from India for the H1B visa. Only 60,000 were issued. It was like tossing a coin; one in two had to go back. Microsoft's application for a visa for Kunal was rejected. He was told to leave in three months.

'That was the second biggest disappointment for me, after the IIT fiasco. That is how it felt at the time. Now it feels like a second blessing in disguise.'

~

Shashank was not known for excelling at academics in his school, Bangalore's National Public School, Rajajinagar. The school put great store by academics, but Shashank excelled at everything that was not academics: plays, dumb charades, volleyball, cricket. He led his house team in many sports.

He was not bad at studies, but average-to-above-average. He thought academics was not what everyone made it out to be. It was what your parents wanted you to do. Shashank aspired to being something other than a schoolkid who did his lessons. He saw himself doing well in other things. It made him popular in school.

This went on till he was in class eleven. As the clock ticked to class twelve, Shashank saw everyone around him put their heads down and bury themselves in studies. It was a sudden, baffling change. Shashank had always been friends with the good students. But when the shift in their attitude happened as they moved to class twelve, Shashank found himself in the bottom 15 percentile of his class.

It was a rude shock. He took pride in doing well at everything about which he cared. He needed to rediscover himself and show his real self in studies, too.

So he locked himself in a room—a shed atop his cousin's house—for almost a year. Away from everything. And he studied. All his friends were surprised, but Shashank shut everything out. He grew a beard and focused on his books, round the clock, day after day, week after week, month after month.

When the class twelve results were issued, Shashank was surprised by his friends' reaction. They were shocked to see him in the top 15 percentile. He did not understand their disbelief. He had always excelled at anything he had put his mind to.

The results, in 2005, paved his way to NIT Surathkal, which is perceived to be just a level below the Indian Institutes of Technology. His peer group there was really good. It had some of the best students from all over the country. They were really competitive, not only in studies but also in everything else. Just like Shashank. They pushed him to work harder.

It was his first time in a hostel. He did all the new things one does when one first goes to live away from home. 'I'm not going into the details, but all the things you explore in hostel life. The overnight trips to Goa, the trekking, everything you were so far not allowed to do.'

He enjoyed his first year, but was bored by the end of it. He was back in the above-average group in academics, focusing more on co-curricular activities.

In the second year he focused on the clubs. They were a new thing for him. He joined two: Ephoria, the entrepreneurship forum, which had just been formed, and the computer science club.

He did everything he could at the two clubs. But was bored of them by the time the year was out. By the time the third year rolled on, Shashank had no wish to do what the other students were doing. He was done with all those activities. That was when the entrepreneurship bug bit him.

Ephoria had entrepreneurs visiting and addressing the students. At one of those sessions, the entire audience perked up when Ajit Balakrishnan, the man behind Rediff, one of India's earliest Internet start-ups, rose to speak. He used simple words where others would employ jargon, trying to sound sophisticated and complicated. Shashank felt energized by Balakrishnan's talk. The way he simplified things made Balakrishnan a cut above the rest.

Balakrishnan ignited Shashank's interest in entrepreneurship when he started describing a set of ideals for entrepreneurs—what today goes by the term First Principles—to boil everything down to the fundamental truths and then reason up from there. It was not about making money or about being a businessman. It was about an entrepreneur having clarity, modesty and a sense of simplicity.

Shashank started ruminating over a couple of ideas—nothing substantive—the way one tends to do in hostels. After dinner, or after midnight, he would sit around and, while talking shop with friends, also throw his ideas into the mix.

Abhinav and he had been in the same circles. They were in the same class at Surathkal. They were two of the four students from their year selected for Ephoria. They had common friends too. But somehow they had never become close till they began to bond during their discussions over doing something on their own. They also did some projects together for Ephoria.

~

Yogendra Vasupal and I meet in Stayzilla's new Bangalore office—its main office is in Chennai—across the road from the BDA Complex in HSR Layout. The office is still being done up. It was nearly empty till a couple of months ago, when a large number of new hires joined.

Yogi greets me warmly, and we sit in a small room with a large window that opens up on to the road and a large rickety table that fills it up. The fan is unusually noisy, the noise being made by the throw of the air, not by any of its moving parts. Yogi is a Kannadiga whose parents had settled down in

Chennai a long time ago. He has these heavy, droopy eyelids. He sniffs frequently and speaks rapidly, even more so when talking about the newspaper headline that changed his life.

'Sold! To eBay! Baazee for Rs 230 cr'.

That headline from the *Economic Times* jumped out at Yogi. He grabbed the paper and ran downstairs. He lived on the second floor with his parents. The ground and first floors were a hospital—Yogi's mother's hospital.

Yogi always referred to their home as 'the hospital'. It was in a desolate place, with houses in the locality spaced 500 metres apart. There was a lot of playing space, but no one to play with. As a child, Yogi used to pray that other children would fall ill and come to the hospital, but not too seriously ill because he wanted to play with them.

The day he ran downstairs with a newspaper in hand, his mother was busy at work, but Yogi had to interrupt her. He pointed to the news item and the photograph of Baazee's co-founder, Avnish Bajaj, and said: 'Look here, people are making money on the Internet. It is possible.'

Yogi always knew how to make money. He knew about shares and debentures at age ten, from his father, who was an economics professor. When he was in class five, stickers that glowed in the dark were quite popular at his school. He would buy a bunch of packets for Rs 25 and sell them loose in his school. It gave him 70 per cent returns, weekly. That worked for eight weeks until the shopkeeper, the only one in the vicinity that sold those stickers, realized what was happening and started selling the stickers loose himself.

From then onwards, Yogi has had an aversion for markets with limited supply. 'That shopkeeper was the only supplier. I ended up creating a market, only for him to move in and claim it.'

In 1999, he joined the computer science course at Anna University, the same engineering college where Mu Sigma's

Dhiraj Rajaram had proposed to Ambiga within thirty days of their becoming classmates. Yogi, though, was focused on other things.

Two months after joining, he bought himself a computer and an Internet connection. Three months later, in the beginning of the year 2000, he began to freelance online, building small websites. By the time the year ended, he was making Rs 20,000 a month.

The college was a five-minute walk from home. Still, in the first year Yogi attended only about 60 per cent of the classes. In the second year, he built a dozen websites and was earning advertising income. One of the sites was for an American senator, which ran polls, and drew thousands of visitors who came to answer the polls. By the end of the second year of college, Yogi was making Rs 40,000 a month. So he stopped going to college, though he did not officially drop out.

His parents did not object. They knew Yogi was not going out and doing strange things; he just stayed home and worked on his computer. And he made money. All they said was that he should not officially quit college, that he could take a year's break.

He did, and found himself spending more time running errands for the household than working on his beloved computer. He figured it was better to have a college he could bunk, and rejoined.

He had lost a year by that time and was now in a class junior to his friends. But that did not make much of a difference because his attendance stayed stubbornly at 5 per cent or so. He would go to college to meet his friends. Back home, he was left alone to work on the computer because he was no longer seen as someone who just stayed home and had a lot of free time.

In 2001, he started doing some work with Amazon, and his income jumped to Rs 70,000 a month. By the final year of college, which was in late 2003, he made an AdWords account, the advertising platform. He started to bid and buy long-tail keywords, which make it possible to bring the person doing a search to more relevant and specific advertising. For instance, if a person searches for 'hotels near HSR Layout in Bangalore for below Rs 300 with dormitory', you can direct the search sites to where there would be ads for hotels in Bangalore near HSR Layout.

By the time Yogi was supposed to graduate from college, he was already making Rs 1 lakh a month. That was a big amount at the time, when one could buy a good house in Chennai for Rs 12 lakh or so.

Yet, Yogi was not content. He was making money, but that was the easy part. He wanted to create value. What he was doing was an online version of trading. He wanted to be more than a trader; he wanted to create something valuable that would endure.

At the end of 2003, he spoke to Rupal Surana and Sachit Singhi, who had become his friends on the very first day of college, and suggested the three of them start their own company. 'Great idea,' said both. 'But what will the company do?'

The sentiment in India had improved. The quick changes of government in the 1990s had given way to a stable one run by the National Democratic Alliance. The technology meltdown was nearing its end. Manufacturing activity was clawing its way back after hitting rock bottom in 2001. The India Shining Campaign was starting.

Great value is created during transition—be it political, economic, or technological. It was the right time.

Yogi and his two friends toyed with the idea of selling books online. His affiliation with Amazon had planted this idea in his head. Besides, Yogi loved books. Every summer holiday, from class seven onwards, he used to intern at a bookshop only to be able to read in peace.

But there was not enough data available on the books trade. The size of the market was a hazy concept, and tie-ups with publishers appeared to be a maze.

So they looked at real estate. There was data on it, since there were guidelines set by the government. Yogi and friends wanted to set up an end-to-end marketplace for real estate. It would cover the entire life cycle of a tenant–owner agreement. The company would deduct the month's rent from the tenant's bank account and send it to the owner. But it turned out to be an idea ahead of its time.

So they started to look at short-term accommodation rather than long-term accommodation, the latter which is real estate. Luckily for them, in 2001, the first post-Independence study on the country's tourism market had been conducted by the ministry of statistics and programme implementation. It estimated the market size at more than $7 billion, a big value at the time.

It was a fragmented market too, with no threat of a giant like the glow stickers shop gobbling away at everybody else. By this time, Yogi was engaged to Rupal. He wanted to be a good boy and convince both his parents and hers that his idea for a new venture was good before going ahead with the wedding. They talked for five months.

Yogi's father asked why he could not simply do real estate. He had several properties in Bhopal, Goa and Chennai— both commercial and residential. Yogi could manage them. But Yogi would have none of it. He told his father to will those properties to someone else. Left to him, he would sell them all and put the money in a start-up.

Rupal's family—the Suranas—was Marwari and open to all kinds of ideas of entrepreneurship, but they were not sure one could make money online. The dotcom bust was still a fresh in memory.

The *Economic Times* article about Baazee won the day for Yogi and friends. Perhaps fittingly, Matrix Partners India went on to invest in their company, and Avnish Bajaj, as its head, sat on their company's board.

~

CHAPTER 3

Avnish Bajaj fell in love with the US at first sight. As a country and society, it was liberating. The university was a breeze—a nice and pleasant one. Avnish did not have to study and yet got straight As. He finished his masters in one year, all thanks to the way his mind was trained under the IIT system. His IIT pedigree had benefited him in some way, after all. Actually, in many ways: 'Whatever I am, it is because of IIT,' he says.

The University of Wisconsin was a great school, but not very well known. Its location, far from USA's corporate and financial hubs, meant that not many marquee companies came to recruit on campus. Microsoft came, and rejected Avnish. He failed its technical test. He received offers from some companies that were not really household names in India, the likes of Random Computers.

One day, one of his professors asked Avnish if he would like to work at Apple Computer. Avnish did not know much about Apple but had heard that it was a bit of a maverick. That was reason enough for him to say yes. The professor picked up the phone, called someone, and told Avnish he was good to go. Avnish was interviewed and given a job on the spot.

Avnish stayed with Apple for the next three-and-a-half years, till the end of 1996. He would be a good source for anyone writing about the company's turbulent history during that period, when it went through four CEOs and became almost bankrupt. Its market capitalization, $546 billion when this book was being finalized, had fallen to $1.5 billion.

Avnish started out as a software engineer at Apple and rose to become programme manager for a project that was a joint venture between Apple and SAP. SAP in those days had only a Windows-based front end. Avnish was part of the team that built SAP's Macintosh-based front end.

Before leaving Apple, Avnish got a chance to make a presentation as part of a product group, before Steve Jobs. Jobs had just come back as the CEO, after Sculley, Amelio, and Spindla had taken turns at the corner office. Despite all the books and articles that have been written about Jobs, it is irresistible to ask anyone who has met him for their impression of him. 'He was clearly a genius. That was obvious. He could be a bit rough around the feathers to deal with. But it was clear he was going to change the industry.' (There! I have my very own second-hand Steve Jobs moment, and you, your third-hand one.)

Despite the promise of change, Avnish was bored with what he was doing. In some way, India kept calling. Software outsourcing out of the country was beginning to catch on. Avnish kept reading about it every now and then. Small but significant work like data entry and medical records were increasingly being done at offshore locations in India by American companies, marking the onset of business process outsourcing. This coincided with Avnish's rising desire to have his own business. Why this desire?

'If I analyse it in retrospect, I was perhaps in a hurry. Perhaps the hunger was to make money. Today, clearly, money is not what drives me. But I think it did at the time. I came from a middle class background to the land of opportunity and I had to make it big.' He was in the valley, where he saw many Indian entrepreneurs doing stuff. 'Why not start to do this data processing thing everyone was so kicked about?' he thought. So he started a company called Soft Magic while at Apple and tried to get some data processing done out of India. He tied up with somebody in India—he cannot even recall the person's name now. Soft Magic did not get many clients. But Avnish loved the sales part. He would pick up the Yellow Pages and call up companies doing data processing to understand how they worked. He did some research, tried to get some clients, made sales pitches.

It was fun, but short-lived. It ended when Avnish realized his H1B visa would not let him do anything other than work with Apple. He did not want to risk deportation.

~

Deported from the US, Kunal Bahl came back to India in September 2007, and called Rohit Bansal.

They were together in classes eleven and twelve at the Delhi Public School, R.K. Puram. They sat next to each other, talked about food, and cracked dirty jokes. They bonded over mathematics.

They had also studied together for the JEE. Kunal cleared the screening with a good rank, but had a rather bad main exam. He did well in maths and chemistry, but did not clear the cut-off in physics.

Rohit got a top 100 rank and joined IIT Delhi. When Kunal returned from the US, Rohit was working with Capital One, the US financial services company, in Bangalore. He had just received his H1B visa to go to the US next year. It had been stamped in his passport—the gateway to a great life.

Kunal told Rohit not to go; that they should start something together in India.

Rohit comes from a small town called Malout, 45 kilometres from Bathinda in Punjab, and is from a modest background. Going to the US would have meant a great opening of doors for him.

Yet, when Kunal called, Rohit simply replied he wouldn't go to the US, that he would stay back in India and build a business with Kunal. That was that. They never talked about it again.

First, they started a coupons business, and called it Money Saver. When Kunal was in the US, he did not have much money, but he loved to eat out. The only way he could afford to do so was by using coupons. This gave him the idea for a similar venture in India. In 2007, organized retail was taking off in India. Kunal and Rohit thought the coupon business was going to become a billion dollar one.

The calculation was simple. There were tens of millions of people who shopped in India. It was not too much to expect that a million people would buy their coupon book every month.

It looked a little more complicated after a year of slumming the streets of Delhi, trying to sign up restaurants, spas and salons to get them into their coupon book. Most of them did not know what a coupon was. To them, Kunal and Rohit were two kids with a PowerPoint presentation, wearing jackets even in the Delhi summer and asking them for a favour.

Naturally, the managers of the restaurants, salons and spas were unkind to the young men. They were made to wait outside even when the managers were not doing anything useful inside. On one occasion, Rohit waited seven hours outside the office of a shoe company because its manager wouldn't take calls or respond to email.

Kunal and Rohit had a calling sheet. They had set up two tables in Kunal's bedroom, which were their work stations. They would take turns to call up the same people. They would call a brand manager or a merchant at least once every two days. 'Did you think about it?' If they didn't respond after three calls, they got a 'standing ovation'. Kunal and Rohit showed up at their office and the manager had to respond either yes or no in person.

The chief marketing officer of a jeans brand stopped taking their calls. He was not available even when they turned up at his office for a standing ovation. So Kunal pulled out a VoIP phone he had retained from his US days and called the CMO's US number. This time, probably thinking the overseas calling number indicated something important, the CMO took the call. Kunal reintroduced himself and asked when he could see him. The CMO said he was leaving for Hong Kong and that Kunal could come see him the next day. That was great, except that, as indicated by the phone number Kunal was calling from, he was supposed to be in the US. Thinking on his feet, he said: 'I am on my way to the airport in New York to catch a plane to Delhi. But I can change my tickets to Bangalore.' The next day, Kunal and Rohit took a flight from Delhi to Bangalore and signed the deal.

~

In 2003–04, Vijay Shekhar Sharma was hardly ever seen at home, not if there was still daylight.

As One97 grew bigger, it needed more money because it was running more servers, bigger teams, and had to pay royalty on the music. But the tech bubble had popped and all technology companies were seen as spoiled children to be straightened out. Finally, the money ran out. So One97 took loans, and then some more loans at higher rates of interest, as high as 24 per cent, and became caught in a vicious cycle.

Any money that came in went into paying the interest, office rent and salaries for the twenty-five people team. Vijay, who paid himself the last, had no money to pay his house rent.

So he would go home only late at night and scale the walls to get into his own house to sleep. He would wake up early in the morning and run away so the landlord would not see him.

His landlord was a rich, genial soul. 'Beta,' he would tell Vijay, 'you should save some money for house rent.'

'Sorry, uncle,' Vijay said each time, 'The problem happened only this month, it will be fine the next month.'

But next month would only be worse, and the time came when Vijay did not have money for food. So he would pile on to friends so he could eat at their place. The paranthewallah near Moolchand Hospital in south Delhi, known for his delicious, low-priced fare served late into the night, became a source of sustenance. Vijay would walk down to it after work, but with an eye on his wallet. Two cups of tea in the winter was a luxury—a far cry from the days of golgappa shots without vodka. 'The circle of life,' says Vijay, with a guffaw.

Some days he would do training or consultancy work to make money. He would go to companies and teach their employees about the Internet. He was paid Rs 1000 for a day of training. For some of the companies, he would set up a website and email while his team ran the One97 operations. The money Vijay earned this way kept One97 going.

While on the training-consultancy circuit, Vijay ran into Piyush Agrawal, whose Polar Software needed help with its technology. Vijay's work took Agrawal's company from no profits to a handsome profit.

'Why don't you become the CEO of my company?' asked Agrawal.

'I can't,' said Vijay, 'I have my own company to run.'

'Think about it,' said Piyush.

And Vijay did.

This was in 2004. Vijay was twenty-six. His parents were frantically looking for a suitable bride for him. But there was a problem.

Vijay's father would initiate negotiations with a girl's family. The girl's side would initially be very keen, given Vijay's status as an electronics and communications graduate from Delhi College of Engineering. Someone from the girl's side would come over to meet him, then things would go very quiet.

Vijay's father was puzzled. But then he figured it out. The girl's side went quiet once they discovered Vijay was not bringing home a guaranteed amount in salary every month. The father was now pushing Vijay to shut down his company and take up a job, one that would pay him at least Rs 30,000 a month. That, the father believed, would be a strong magnet to fetch him a good girl. He also ticked off Vijay for having taken loans from friends and family. 'I don't like it,' he would say.

All this would bring tears to Vijay's eyes. He had given his blood and sweat to One97; he could not bear to shut it down. But he could no longer stave off his father's nagging.

So he spoke to Piyush Agrawal.

'Why don't I work for you half a day every day and you pay me Rs 30,000 a month? I will be your CEO, but only for half of the working day.'

For Piyush, it was a steal. He was getting a CEO who had brought his company into profits even while working as an outsider. Now he was ready to go full-time. So what if it was for only half the working day? Whoever got a good CEO for Rs 30,000 a month?

The deal was done. Vijay told his family he had become a CEO and was earning Rs 30,000 a month. In 2005, Vijay got married to a girl from Jaipur.

The wedding was a simple affair. It had to be, since Vijay had no cash flow and he did not want his parents or his wife's parents to spend on the wedding. The budget had to be kept within Rs 2 lakh, which he had had borrowed from a chap who was his partner in XS Corps, his first company.

He has a delightful little son now, on whom he dotes, and who visits him at office from time to time and sits in his lap. But Vijay is still not sure that getting married was the right thing to do.

'The spouse has a lot of expectations from a new relationship. But I could not devote time to my wife even if I wanted to.'

All his time was spent trying to keep One97 going, which was becoming difficult with each passing day.

One day, Piyush Agrawal asked Vijay what his company did and why it needed so much of his time. Vijay told him about One97's business of systems and content, how the content was delivered to the consumer through texts and calls, and how the money was charged by the operator and shared with One97.

'How can I help?' asked Piyush.

'Give me a loan of Rs 8 lakh,' said Vijay. 'That is the amount of loan I need to repay.'

'I cannot give you Rs 8 lakh just to repay your loan. But I can invest this amount in your company,' said Piyush.

That he did, and also gave space in his office to One97 so Vijay could be close to both Polar and One97 at the same time. In return, Piyush got a 40 per cent stake in One97.

Piyush sold most of his stake later for Rs 87 crore. That should be enough to make him one of the shrewdest investors in the history of India. But had he held on . . . well . . . One97, with its ownership of the Paytm mobile wallet and an online marketplace, is now valued at billions of dollars. It also has a payments bank licence now.

The high current valuation makes some people question Vijay's wisdom in giving away 40 per cent for just Rs 8 lakh and some office space. They forget that the value of money depends on the need it serves. Had Piyush's Rs 8 lakh not come in at the time it did, One97 may have shut down and there would be no Paytm. In a sense, Piyush's money was Vijay's angel round of funding.

Later, Polar sold its office and moved. And still later, when Vijay had the money, he bought back the same office.

'This is the Polar Software building,' he says, moving his hand in a sweeping gesture.

The circle of life!

~

Rupal Surana and Sachit Singhi completed their engineering degree in 2005. Rupal joined Convergys, and then Infosys. She left Infosys to join Yogi at Inasra Technologies, the company the three of them had registered in Chennai in 2005.

Sachit had been in love with a girl from the time both were in class three. The girl came from a no-nonsense, Tamil–Brahmin family. There was only one way to get her family to accept Sachit in their fold. It was the lengthy way, which Sachit happily took. After graduating from Anna University, he went on to do an MBA, got a job at Tata Business Support and got engaged to the girl. Not even a month had passed after the engagement when he told his prospective father-in-law that he wanted to leave the job and set up his own company. That in reality he had already been working part-time at his company.

The father-in-law took it on the chin. 'It is a done deed. What to do! Go ahead.'

With the blessings of the families, Yogi, Rupal and Sachit shot out of the blocks, and ran into a wall.

They talked to owners and managers of holiday properties and accommodation services—hotels, motels, lodges, guesthouses, anyone willing to rent out space for the short-term—about how they operated. The idea was to bring them all online. But few of the property owners and managers knew what a computer did. Only the large hotel people had some idea, which was that you could put a DVD in it to watch movies.

Yogi is a Kannadiga from Chikmagalur based in Chennai, Rupal a Marwari from the Rajasthan-Gujarat border, Sachit half-Marwari and half-Telugu. Together, they could speak several languages. They used every language they could to convince the property owners—starting with the large hotels—that they could get more customers on the Internet.

At twenty-three, the three looked so young that people often indulged them. They looked like children who would forget all about the business once they went back home.

They did not. They came back, again and again. They said they did not want any payment upfront, and that they would sign a contract on commission. Many properties began to sign the contract just to get rid of them.

By the time 2007 rolled in, they had signed contracts with 500 properties. At this time, Airbnb, the US-based company that has become the biggest in this business worldwide, had not been founded.

In 2007, Inasra (*asara* is Hindi for shelter, 'in' was for India) went up as a beta site. It went completely live in August that year, with 1100 properties. It grew 50 per cent year on year and became self-sustaining by 2009. It had taken no external investment; Yogi's other activities that earned Rs 1 lakh a month funded it in the early years.

Still, it was a trifle too early to the market. In every country, they noticed, the travel vertical had taken off online, but not accommodation. Probably because there was no standard reference rate—a room for Rs 800 could vary drastically in quality between different countries.

A few investors became interested in Inasra, but they said: 'Add flights. Stay *mein koi game nahi hai*.' (There is not much business in stays.)

But Yogi would not have that. He did not want a repeat of the sticker seller story. With twenty-two players, the online travel market in India looked fragmented, but supply was dominated by the two or three leading airlines. 'How am I going to stop them from competing with you? Where is the balance of power?' he wondered.

Inasra focused on stays, and therefore got no funding. That meant no marketing or branding. What it did have, though, was time on the hands of its founders. They used it to increase the supply—get more and more properties online. The theory was that when the market did reach an inflection point, it would veer towards the one with the largest supply.

There are different kinds of marketplaces. For some, the buyer and seller have to be in the same city, such as the case for Bhavish Aggarwal's Ola. For some, they can be either in the same city or a different one, such as for eBay. For Inasra, the buyer and seller were almost always in different cities—only in rare cases would one book a room for a few days in the city where one lives.

So Inasra could not follow a city-specific model. On the contrary, it required width—properties covering large swathes of cities, towns and tourist hotspots. For instance, Inasra would have only fifty-odd properties in Bangalore, for those visiting the city. But it would also have properties in some thirty towns within a five-hour journey of Bangalore, where the people of Bangalore might look for accommodation when they travelled.

Inasra listed properties in 110 cities in 2009. Doubling that number pushed up bookings by a measly 30 per cent. It was disheartening, but only until Inasra acquired critical mass. Today, if it increases supply or cities by a mere 10 per cent, bookings jump five-fold.

'A lot of questions keep popping up in one's mind. Am I on the right track? I am putting in so much effort, is this even meaningful? It starts to mess with your head. The key thing is to be consistent, patient and persistent,' says Yogi.

From 2009 onwards, Inasra began to generate cash flows. It did business worth Rs 90 lakh that year. By now it had a seven-member team. It had taken no seed funding, and no angel funding either. Rs 90 lakh was enough to begin with.

Now it wanted to spend on marketing. So the founders took money from their parents, parents-in-law, brothers-in-law, drinking buddies and friends from school and college. 'I have twenty-five friends and family who have equity in our company. I work for them. I am too lazy to work for myself.'

The founders also took their time to have their children. Yogi and Rupal had their first child, a daughter, on 9 September 2009 or 09.09.09. They planned another child, aiming for 10.10.10, but missed it by a month. The son was born in November 2010.

Around this time, they rebranded Inasra. The name did not fully capture the company's character. Many of their repeat customers called it 'Insara' and that rankled. The company was making some money. It called in consultants and told them that customers were not getting the name right.

Change the name, said the consultants. The new name had to communicate that the company could get you any room for any budget in any district, or zilla, as a district is called in Hindi. For people abroad, it had to be the Godzilla of stays. There were nine other suggestions for a new name, but Stayzilla stuck.

The team started 2011 by launching the new brand. By the middle of the year, growth had touched 50 per cent and continued year on year. The company was also gaining scale. In the financial year 2011-12, it did business of Rs 2.5 crore. It now had a twenty-member team.

It was getting easier to get properties on board. The founders' thinking was simple: if there is a room somewhere to let out, they would feature it online and sell it. Without anyone consciously realizing it, Stayzilla had become the marketplace for stays. The new element of 'alternative stays'—mainly home stays—got added, especially in places like Coorg. The market had a momentum of its own. This looked as good a time as any to raise capital.

They started speaking to investors and met 'Ravi Sir'—Ravindra Krishnappa of the Indian Angel Network. Conversation flowed. They liked each other, and Ravi Sir took the proposal to the IAN angels. Stayzilla raised half-a-million dollars from thirty-nine IAN members, who had invested individually. At the time it was doing forty room-nights a day.

The money came in April 2012, making possible the much-needed marketing. By December 2012, Stayzilla was doing 250 room-nights a day, and by December 2013, 750. By December 2014, room-night bookings had soared to 4000 a day.

The reason for this exponential growth was that marketing and supply were now in conjunction. By March 2012, the company had 2000 properties, which doubled by December, increasing to 5500 by next December, and nearly quadrupled by December 2014. In March 2015, when Yogi and I met, Stayzilla had 25,000 properties. Alternative stays, which constituted 5 per cent of the business in January 2014, accounted for 40 per cent of the business by December 2014.

This focus on supply was brought in by Avnish Bajaj, whose Matrix Partners invested in Stayzilla in June 2013.

~

Suchi Mukherjee's senior director—who told her to send someone else in her place for her own wedding because, after all, she had dated by proxy and could just as well get married by proxy as well—was not entirely correct. But he was not altogether wrong.

Suchi had not dated by proxy, but the dating sure had been long-distance. But distance was not the reason it took Sandeep two years to get Suchi to agree to marry him.

Suchi's father believed that movies were a waste of time. Suchi watched her first movie—Richard Attenborough's *Gandhi*—at thirteen. A couple of years later her mother made her watch Hrishikesh Mukherjee's *Abhimaan*, in which a couple breaks up because the wife becomes a more sought-after singer than the husband and is paid more.

'Boss, what if I start earning more than you?' Suchi had asked Sandeep.

'Are you mad?' Sandeep had shot back. 'My family is run by women.'

His mother was dean of French at Jawaharlal Nehru University. She was also Indira Gandhi's French tutor and interpreter for the Government of India. Two of the mother's sisters were senior government officers, and a third was a well-known gynaecologist.

'But what if I come home later than you do?' Suchi persisted.

The coming home part had not figured in their two-year courtship. Sandeep was with Monitor, the management consultancy, in Boston, and Suchi with Lehman in London. Initially, she had planned to move to the US, but at Lehman she was told that whatever semblance of life she had would be lost in New York, so chaotic was a finance professional's life in that city.

So they maintained this trans-Atlantic dating, and made the time difference work in their favour. Suchi would stay in office till 2 a.m. in the early morning, which was 10 p.m. at night for Sandeep. And they would chat. It took two years of that for Suchi to agree to the marriage. But she warned

Sandeep: *'Bete, shaadi mein kuchh nahi milega.'* He was not going to get any dowry.

She showed up for the wedding just two days before. She told her mother she wanted only one sari to wear at the wedding, and informed her mother-in-law she wanted one sari for the reception. There would not be anything else exchanged between the two families.

When her father married her mother, he was handed a Rolex by the grandmother. The mother's family was poor, but the Rolex was an heirloom that had survived. 'I can't give you much, but here is this watch,' the grandmother had said.

Suchi's father refused to take it. 'One day,' he said, 'when I have children and if they are girls, I don't expect to give anything when they get married.'

Suchi kept her father's word. Her reward was that her father refused to do *kanyadan*. He did not like the concept of having to 'give away' his daughter. 'The whole concept of kanyadan is that my daughter is no longer my responsibility. But my child is independent. She is not to be given away in a *daan*.'

The father's non-linear thinking and his belief in doing things differently are embedded in LimeRoad, the company Suchi founded. But it would be many years before she got there.

~

For the first nine months, Mu Sigma was a one-man company. That period of going it alone was the best gift Dhiraj Rajaram could have hoped for, because you think differently when you are sitting all by yourself. Solitude forces you to really think. Company-building—truly building a company—is a lonely pursuit, like writing, or any other creative process.

Dhiraj's obsession nursed Mu Sigma during those months. Mu was designed to help companies institutionalize data-driven decision-making. The flow is from data, to data engineering (technology), to data sciences (a combination of mathematics and technology), and to decision sciences (which combine business, mathematics, technology, behavioural sciences, and design thinking). The whole equation constitutes decision support.

A leading technology company and a large insurance company in the US signed up as clients almost at the same time the company needed more people to come on board. Finally, Dhiraj found a companion when Sayandeb Banerjee joined in June 2005 from GE.

Once Mu Sigma had propelled its start, it never looked back. Today it works with 140 Fortune 500 customers and is nudging a quarter of a billion dollars in revenue. That is big. Still, it continues to grow at nearly 50 per cent every year. Like a start-up.

The company is unique in other ways too. If you look at the other successful start-ups, they are versions of ventures that have already worked well in the United States or some other country. Flipkart is the Amazon of India, InMobi is the Admob of India and MakeMyTrip India's Expedia.

Mu Sigma is an original. There is just one other outfit that comes close to what it does: Palantir, a data mining juggernaut funded by the Central Intelligence Agency of the United States. With the exception of Palantir, Mu Sigma is the only company that integrates art (on the part of the business analyst), science (brought in by the applied mathematician) and scale (achieved by programmers).

At the outset, Mu Sigma had the approach of a true start-up, intent on breaking convention and doing something altogether new. It also practised what it preached: embracing change.

IBM and Accenture could have done it earlier and on a larger scale than Mu Sigma. But, being large organizations set in their ways, they could only think of topping up whatever they were already doing—which was information technology. Their mindset was, 'We have a horse carriage, let's yoke more horses to it.'

Mu Sigma considered itself a car and, therefore, decided it must be thought of differently from a horse carriage. Booz Allen, too, where Dhiraj had first got the idea, had not thought much about it. All it saw in Dhiraj was a youth in his twenties jumping up and down about an idea that sounded obtuse. He would have been happy had Booz Allen done it, but is now glad it did not. The idea has, after all, led to the creation of his own company.

What Mu Sigma does—help people make decisions—is drilled into its name. To make good decisions, you need to ask good questions, and you need to be confident enough about the answers to take action on them. That comes from 'mean' (Mu) and 'standard deviation' (Sigma).

The *Economic Times,* in April 2014, reported on the company's screening session for engineers who wanted to join its team of 'decision scientists'. They were asked to create a business model for a seller of *vada pav,* Mumbai's favourite street snack that wraps a potato cutlet in a bun. The aspirants had to collate data on the price of all the ingredients, the political situation, cyclones and other forces of nature, and make sense of them.

~

The Texas Instruments office in Bangalore was next door to Motorola's, where a friend of Phani's worked. This friend told Phani to approach TiE, The Indus Entrepreneurs, a large, global network of Indian entrepreneurs.

Phani hadn't heard of it. He googled it, signed up for a membership and attended one of its fortnightly sessions. There he came to know that TiE was launching an entrepreneurship acceleration programme. Phani, Charan and Sudhakar applied for it, made a presentation, and got, Sanjay Anandaram, who would go on to mentor them for the next seven years.

I met Sanjay in a charming cafe just down the road from Flipkart's office in Koramangala. He is well-groomed, thoughtful, measured and recognized. The cafe people know him, as does the young lady on the next table. That's no surprise, because Sanjay does a lot of pro bono mentoring of start-ups. After a while, the young lady cannot contain herself and comes over to talk to Sanjay. He listens patiently, and gives her his Gmail ID.

He had showed similar patience when he stepped into the picture at redBus. He liked the young founders, but had to raise fundamental questions. 'Why are you pushing your software if the bus operators do not want it? They have mastered their processes and have been running them for decades. You are three young guys asking them to change all their processes and use your software. Why will they? What are they getting out of it? You say it will improve their processes and someday get them more customers. But that cannot be demonstrated today. Ask them what they want. What they really, really want. And try to figure out a solution.'

Phani, Sudhakar and Charan thought there was no harm in doing what Sanjay suggested. They were not making any headway anyway. So they went to the bus operators and asked them what they wanted.

'Nothing,' said the operators, 'Certainly not your software. We work through agents; they get us customers.'

The penny dropped. All the operators wanted was to sell their seats. Nothing else.

The three turned to their mentor again. 'We will not give software to bus operators,' they told Sanjay. 'We will instead make a B2C website and drive sales.'

Sanjay agreed. 'The biggest thing is to make sales. Everything else will fall in place.'

So they scrapped the software meant for operators and wrote a new one, which went on to become redBus.in, India's most successful website for bus ticketing.

Now they had a new challenge. They no longer had to sell software to bus operators; they had to sell seats to travellers.

They started by providing static information on the site. There is an AC bus leaving at this time from this place, and this is the price of a ticket from this place to that place. If a customer wanted to buy a ticket, he or she would click on an icon that would open up a form showing the number of seats available on the bus, with a field for entering the buyer's phone number. Once the request form was filled and submitted, Phani and friends would call the operator and book the seat. They would then call the customer, provide him or her with the seat details and collect the money.

They were acting like travel agents, but without the benefit of having their customers sitting across the table from them, and therefore without the opportunity of taking instant views or money. Later they began to block some seats and put them live on the website. If the customer saw available seats, she could book them instantly; they did not need to provide their phone number. This arrangement only required that the bus operator commit to not selling the seats he had given to redBus until all his other seats were sold out. Some of the large operators agreed to this condition.

As the three entrepreneurs learned the business, they realized that most buses had only 80 per cent occupancy during the non-holiday season, and that most of the seats were sold on the day of the journey. So they changed their pitch. They told the operators: 'Give us 20 per cent of your seats. And keep them for us until your other seats are sold out.'

Rajesh Travels was the first to block 20 per cent of its bus seats for them. But like the other operators, it covered only a small number of routes out of the hundreds that connect Bangalore to towns and cities. If someone travelling to Chennai found no buses available to the city on the website, he would go away disappointed. This would make for bad word-of-mouth publicity.

redBus needed to find a way to pick out those customers from the crowd who needed tickets for the routes they did have listed on their portal.

It struck them that everywhere people lived in community clusters. Even in Delhi, nearly every locality that had been settled for a while—such as Rajendra Nagar, Patel Nagar, Model Town or Chittaranjan Park—had a strong community identity. So too, in Bangalore. People from Kerala stayed in a place called Madiwala; hardly anyone there spoke Kannada. C.V. Raman Nagar is where the migrants lived. In Hyderabad, Phani's parents stayed in Bogampalli, Secunderabad, which is as different from Hi-Tech City as biryani is from pasta.

The new mantra was to figure out the pockets relevant to the routes available on redBus and advertise accordingly, so that visitors on the site ended up finding what they were looking for. As a corollary, those who did not have their routes on redBus would hardly ever hear about it—the result would be more fulfilment, less disappointment and a high conversion rate of visitors to buyers.

Gradually, without a big-bang launch, redBus grew in popularity, and so did the routes it had to offer. But it did not move away from its philosophical moorings. It gave everyone access to its inventory of routes and tickets. 'We did not start from a profit motive. The reason we started this was to sort out the bus ticketing system.'

As the site reached critical mass, it took off in a big way, because things like customer support were already in place. Agents, who had at first ignored them, began to say that redBus was misleading people. When that did not work, they said it was taking away their livelihood.

The founders discussed this with their mentor and board. Were they really robbing people of their livelihood? Not really, both board and mentor said. The march of technology is inevitable. The advent of the automobile put the horse cart out of business. Was that a bad thing?

redBus charged the standard commission from bus operators, regardless of the season and the number of seats it sold for them. This told the operators, who were now selling a large portion of their tickets on the site, that they need not fear it. That the redBus guys won't walk into their office one fine day and demand double the commission. Some operators offered a higher commission so that they could get preferential treatment. But they were turned down. They had to win on customer care.

Still, it was funny that these were the same operators who at one time used to look through Phani and his friends.

~

Every summer break, Abhinav Lal would either go home to Bihar or do an internship somewhere. But he decided to spend the summer of 2008 with Shashank in Bangalore. They wanted to do something together. They ended up creating a company.

At first they were not really serious about it. They did it in the manner of a project, one out of a bunch of things they were trying their hands at that summer. Placement time at

NIT Surathkal was round the corner. They were going to take up jobs. The start-up ecosystem was next to nothing back then. Very few had started a company and made it big.

Abhinav and Shashank, both computer science students, loved the Internet. It was so full of possibilities that a job as an analyst at Goldman Sachs—Shashank's original aspiration—appeared a pale alternative. Pursuing his original interest, Shashank had done an internship in stock markets at the end of his first year at Surathkal. While others were fascinated with Google and Microsoft, Shashank read books on the stock market for which he thought up technology applications. That was the Warren Buffett kind of way, he thought.

The internship woke him up from the Goldman dream. It bored him, and taught him that the stock market worked in ways very different from what he had imagined—not very scientific.

The Internet seemed to have a lot of science behind it, and there was no end to what you cold do with it. Besides, setting up a company felt like just the kind of thing Shashank loved doing—something people wouldn't understand, something out of the ordinary.

Through the Internet, Shashank and Abhinav learned what was happening in the United States. Facebook was gaining ground. Twitter had just launched. India, in comparison, seemed far behind. That became a handicap for it in several areas, including basic or essential matters like medical care.

Shashank's father was to undergo a knee surgery. But his family wanted a second opinion. They found a doctor in the US through his mother's side of the family. The father's records were to be sent to this doctor. Shashank, being the technology kid, was entrusted with sending them.

He took pictures of the files with his camera phone, transferred them to his laptop, attached them to a new message on Gmail, and sent them to the doctor.

But the pictures were not very legible. And the file transfer to and from the doctor's systems was getting stuck.

'I don't have an email button,' said the doctor.

Shashank was stunned. 'That was like three lines of code, and I could write those three lines of code.'

He did so, with Abhinav. They hacked something and gave it to the doctor: an email button and some other cool features he could use. The doctor loved it.

Shashank and Abhinav felt empowered. They asked the doctors in Bangalore whether they had come across the same problem. They had. Technology had not entered healthcare, with the result that consumers were suffering. Both doctors and patients would benefit if there was a system which, like Facebook, could consolidate all the health records of a patient in one place.

Shashank and Abhinav looked at what companies in the United States were doing about this. There were a couple attempting the same thing as them. But they saw a flaw in the others' approach. They were trying to get the patients to upload all their records, which was not going to happen. A patient is not going to come back from a hospital and say, 'Hey, let me upload all my records.' Shashank and Abhinav thought the best way was to get the doctors to enter the records themselves and make them accessible to patients. The patients could use the portal to just view them.

The odds against the two greenhorns were immense. They were two kids in a room in Bangalore saying they knew better than the large tech companies in the United States because they had a paper napkin with a diagram that they were convinced was correct and logical. (Yes, the whole Practo business was first drawn up by Shashank on a tissue paper.)

That's exactly how it panned out. Those two companies in the US shut down and Practo is still flourishing. In 2015 alone, it raised $120 million and announced four acquisitions

by September. The company had earlier been named Naabo
Medical Solutions, but was renamed Practo once it had its
product in place. The new name reflects the company's core
activity. Its most important requirement was to get doctors
online. Everything else would follow. What was most
important for doctors was their practice. But 'practice', 'doc',
or 'health' would have been boring names. Practo was a cool
name to put the doctors' practice online.

~

FashionClues grew rapidly to 75,000 readers in fifty countries,
but at the wrong time. Starting in 2007, it raised a bit of angel
money, but could not raise more. The reason that halted
FashionClues is the same that hobbled many other start-ups.
With the collapse of Lehman Brothers on 15 September 2008,
the global financial markets went into a tizzy, and every kind
of funding dried up. FashionClues had to be shut down in the
middle of 2009.

'It could have done really well. But, typically, for any
start-up, capital is the largest risk. FashionClues needed a
small amount, half-a-million dollars, for customer and reader
acquisition,' says Radhika. But small though it might be, the
money was critical.

A little before Radhika and I met, Clues Network Inc., the
company that owns ShopClues.com, had raised $100 million
from a group of investors led by Tiger Global, which is also
behind Flipkart, India's largest e-retail company.

You have come a long way from the time you failed to
raise half a million, I tell Radhika.

'Oh my God, yes! The failures always help.'

She credits husband Sandeep with making the journey
possible. 'He says, "just do it". He is the one who came up
with the idea for ShopClues.'

While working as an Internet analyst on Wall Street, Sandeep covered MakeMyTrip, Deep Kalra's start-up, that did an IPO on the New York Stock Exchange. One of the earliest analysts to cover the company, Sandeep was in regular touch with Kalra. In September 2010, Sandeep wrote the *India Internet Report*, perhaps the first such by a mainstream Wall Street analyst. He came to India that year as a keynote speaker at an Internet conference. He realized things were moving quite fast here, and foresaw the opportunity in e-commerce. It excited him, drove him.

In January 2011, Sandeep created the first business plan for ShopClues. Radhika joined him in March and started working on marketing, branding and product categories. Sanjay came in that summer.

Sanjay's older daughter and Radhika's older son had been classmates since pre-school in Fremont. They had been friends since then, often hanging out together.

Sanjay and Sandeep met for the first time when Radhika hosted a dinner at her house in 2008. When they were introduced, their names seemed familiar to each other. It so happened that Sandeep also tracked eBay, where Sanjay worked and received his reports.

The rest of the night they talked e-commerce, and found they shared many thoughts about how it should be done. They also shared the same frustration that really no one was doing it right.

Sandeep and Mrinal had known each other for a while and had developed a mutual liking for each other. They had, however, not worked together. Their connection was also in part due to Mrinal's approach to technology. He views technology through the prism of business, and does not consider it an esoteric pursuit as some guys tend to.

Once the team came together, Sandeep went out into the market looking for money and got a really good term sheet from a big VC, the one that called on the evening of 2 August 2011 to say it was pulling out of its commitment to fund their project.

They wriggled out of the hole that phone call had dug for them, only to fall into the hands of a Gurgaon civil contractor who ran away with their money.

~

CHAPTER 4

When the time came to shift to Gurgaon, Radhika was the first to come down, in May 2011. She went through the nightmare of setting up their company, Clues Network, through the Registrar of Companies. It had taken just one day to set up the parent company, as a Delaware corporation.

Radhika ran around for four weeks to get the required permissions for the wholly-owned Indian subsidiary. She put everything in place and made sure the team had a premises to move into immediately when they arrived: the office and corporate housing for the three families. She went back to California in July.

Sandeep–Radhika and Sanjay arrived in Gurgaon in August, and Mrinal in September. In October they moved into their own office in Gurgaon, a shell of a space out there in the boondocks, in the middle of a village.

They got a contractor to build the office. He asked for an advance of Rs 9 lakh to buy the materials and hire labourers. He was given the money, and the flooring work began. The next morning, the founders came to inspect the new floor and found it to be terrible, and very different from the one the contractor had promised. They waited for him to turn up, but he did not. They called him, but the call would not go through. It took several hours for them to realize they had lost their money and their contractor.

'He thought we were a bunch of NRIs who know shit about things.'

Well, he was right, wasn't he?

'Yes, he was right,' Radhika laments.

Out there in the middle of a Gurgaon village, in a shabby office with half-done flooring and duct tape strewn all over, the ShopClues founders decided to take matters into their own hands. The second floor of the building was their office and the basement was to be the warehouse. The founders worked on the entire space with their own hands, cleaning and scrubbing every inch of it. The only NRI-like thing they did was to make videos of themselves getting the office ready.

They worked out of that office for nearly three years, moving to a much more vibrant locality in Sector 44, near the Fortis Hospital, in Gurgaon in August 2014.

By this time, word had spread that a bunch of NRIs was setting up an 'online Karol Bagh'. They were clear from the beginning about that. ShopClues was to be an online marketplace for mainly unstructured categories.

'We wanted to pick up how India truly shopped, and take it online.'

In 2011, most of the e-commerce outfits were like malls rather than the markets that most Indians shop in.

Radhika has a masi—mother's sister—living in Gurgaon. The aunt used to live in Green Park earlier, smack in the heart of New Delhi. The other day her microwave stopped working. Radhika advised her to buy one from a Croma store next door; she just had to walk across to it. But the masi would have none of it; she would buy it from nowhere but her old shop in Aurobindo Place, one among a cluster of shops near Green Park, because the shopkeeper knew her. *Main toh wahin jaoongi, Aurobindo Place, woh banda mujhe jaanta hai.*

That, to Radhika, is the characteristic of the Indian consumer. 'Look at clothes, Indian women's clothes. If we are not talking brands, they go to Sarojini and Lajpat to buy them.'

True, but that did not make an online marketplace any easier to organize. Books—the segment that earned Flipkart its first claim to fame—are easy to sell online, easy to catalogue, easy to ship (they do not break), and easy to receive (you know you have got what you bought).

Try doing that in fashion, or in home and kitchen products. People buy regional brands from the local markets. How many Indians really go to the mall to buy stuff? They visit them mainly for the air conditioning, a low-priced ice cream scoop, and maybe a movie.

'That is the mass market. That is my customer, the one who would spend half a day at the mall and spend Rs 20 on an ice cream, which too is an indulgence because he has bought a branded product. Anything more expensive has to be planned.'

The only model they wanted to follow was that of a marketplace—a decision that the Indian reality only reaffirmed.

The business plan was drawn up in California. There were forty-three million small and medium companies in India, a third of which sold goods. ShopClues wanted to bring all of them online to create the largest selection of products of regional and local brands. This would bring the mass market online. In the process, they would tap the tier-2 and tier-3 towns, where the mass market would strike the strongest chord. This could very well be done, since the mobile phone was already taking a lot more Indians online, as much in the small towns as in the big cities.

Radhika and her partners studied the various models that had worked in other countries, and identified two as the ones to follow: Alibaba's Taobao in China and MercadoLivre in Brazil. A lot of this knowledge resided with Sandeep. That had been his job—to cover the Internet space internationally.

Then Sanjay came in, with thorough product and technology experience of a large marketplace platform at eBay. Mrinal brought in the technology skills. Radhika brought in the customer experience. They complemented one another without stepping on one another's toes.

They were intent on a model that was scalable, which was critical. There was an unidentified, undiscovered market for e-commerce in India. ShopClues wanted to be the online Walmart of India.

It worked. ShopClues was the thirty-fifth to do e-commerce in India, but now features among the top four— after Flipkart, Snapdeal and Amazon—in value of goods sold. It does formidable volumes, with 250,000 merchants selling 6500 different categories of products.

'No one is our real competition. If you are looking for a product that can be legally sold online, you should be able to find it on ShopClues. If you are looking for a bug swatter—the insect killing racquet, which buzzes flies . . . it is disgusting'—Radhika shivers a little—'but if you are looking for one, you will not go to a mall to buy it. You will go to your sector market. Online, where will you buy it? On ShopClues. As you will an emergency light. In clothes, if you are looking for a large selection of white shirts at Rs 300 apiece, you should be able to find it on ShopClues. If you are looking for the lowest price on a 32-inch television, you might find it there.'

I suspect Kunal Bahl will have something to say about this, but there was one item available for sale on ShopClues that took the cake in the 2015 festival season. It was cow-dung cake, which Indians use for pujas. It must have sold like hotcakes, for when I looked it up on 20 October, it was sold out.

~

One morning in 2006, Vijay Shekhar Sharma woke up and switched on a news channel. It showed an office building, a small one in Connaught Place, on fire. It took a few seconds for Vijay to realize it was his office. He still does not know what caused the fire. He guesses it must have been a short circuit.

The fire forced him to move into a small office. The positive outcome of it, as Vijay sees it, was that the smaller space forced him to buy laptops for his people. Otherwise, in every other way, the fire had showed awful timing.

One97 was growing with the telecom industry. Its team had expanded. It installed more servers. It needed more software. Whatever money it made was ploughed back into the business. It needed more money. But money remained as elusive as ever. 'The problem in this country,' says Vijay, 'is that you don't get loans.'

ICICI gave him some money, but it was good to cover only the working capital for some time. It did not help that lending agencies were still more enamoured by a company's pedigree than an entrepreneur's ability and vision. And then the fire happened.

It took a while for Vijay to resume his quest for funds. But nothing had changed in the interim. A potential investor told Vijay that everyone worthy of raising money had already raised it. Another said: 'One97? What's that? Never heard of it.' And yet another snapped: 'Sharma? I don't have the time to meet this guy.'

The investment banker trying to help Vijay raise money would tell potential investors: 'Look, please meet this guy. If you don't like him, I am fine with it. But please spend some time with him.' Very few had the time for Vijay. Those who did had very little of it.

'A typical money-raising meeting would go like this,' says Vijay, changing his voice to make it sound affected and pompous to imitate a potential investor he had met in a hotel lobby. 'Look, I will wake up at 7 a.m. I will get ready by 8 a.m.; 8.30 a.m. is when I go down to the restaurant for breakfast. Can see you me at eight in the lobby area?'

Of course Vijay would be there well before eight. Of course he would not be invited to breakfast but have to make his pitch right there in the lobby. The conversation would be more like a job interview, not like a chat between two persons looking to do business together.

Slowly, some investors began to see merit in what Vijay was trying to do. Sanjeev Aggarwal of Helion Ventures was one of them. 'We need people like you who have built a $5 million company out of the Rs 5 lakh they had saved,' Aggarwal told Vijay.

His sympathetic words touched Vijay. 'Thank you, sir,' he said, his eyes misting over. 'For so many years I was the school topper. I used to get awards. But it has been many years since anyone said anything good about me. Even my family does not like what I am doing. So this means a lot to me.'

Finally, towards the end of 2006, Vijay signed an agreement with Saif Partners, which moved the fastest among those who had shown interest, for $6 million. The money came in March 2007. Vijay had used it up by December.

He needed to raise more money. This was now the second half of 2008. A large fund house said it would do a large round with Vijay: $40 million. That was twice what he was looking for. The large investor said it would also help him forge alliances with big telecom operators. 'We talk to big CEOs.'

Vijay could not believe his luck. 'Wow! Does a deal get any better than this?'

Turned out, it was not such a great deal. This large investor wanted to ride roughshod over those who had given

Vijay money during his times of need. 'Do you want to screw us?' one of Vijay's earlier investors asked him.

No, he did not. He said thanks, but no thanks, to the large investor in August 2008. A month later, Lehman Brothers collapsed and financial markets all over the world fell into turmoil. Funding dried up. Until serendipity reared its pretty head again.

Vijay was speaking at an event in Mumbai where an executive of Intel Capital, the corporate venture capital arm of chipmaker Intel, was in the audience. The executive liked what he heard, and sought Vijay out after the talk. They spoke over coffee. And Intel Cap agreed to invest in spite of the downturn. In dollar terms, it brought in the same amount that had been promised by the big investor whom Vijay had turned down.

~

All the hustling got the big brands to sign up with Money Saver, but Kunal and Rohit could not get as many consumers as they had hoped for. They were sure of selling millions of coupons, but ended up selling no more than 20,000.

This was in 2008–09. They had no money for marketing. They had taken up an office—their first—in the basement of a house in Kirti Nagar's furniture market. It was a Sikh neighbourhood. Every morning when they came in to work, the neighbourhood would ring with a chorus of voices—of mothers calling the Chintus and Buntys down for breakfast, of people in the bustle of setting out for work, school or college and their little spats over parking or manoeuvring their vehicles out.

Recruitment in the early days was done by first getting Kunal's sister-in-law to call from her home prospects in the Naukri.com database. When the candidate reached Kirti

Nagar, the sister-in-law would say she was working from home that day but would guide the candidate to the office. 'There is this black gate, take the left, you will come to a blue house—not that, there is a yellow house after that—a *presswallah* is there in the lane, take the right, go to the basement and press the bell.' Kunal and Rohit would then emerge to do the interview.

Many hires from those early days are still with the company. They are also quite wealthy, with all the stocks that were given out in the early days. The legal entity has remained the same—Jasper Infotech—even as the business has changed several times and is now known as Snapdeal.

One of the first changes the company made was to introduce mobile coupons, the founders having realized the limitations of the physical coupon because of its perishability. The company also started a discount card service. These offers were moderately successful. The big success came only with Snapdeal's launch in February 2010. Until then, it wasn't pretty.

In June 2009, Jasper had to pay Rs 5 lakh in salaries on the seventh of the month. The day before payday, Kunal and Rohit realized there was just Rs 50,000 in the bank because some payments had not come in yet. Together they had Rs 5 lakh in personal savings.

'We went all in,' says Kunal, the use of gambler's language perhaps an indication of his mindset at the time. Having paid the salaries using their savings, they were left with Rs 21,000—Rs 10,000 with Kunal and Rs 11,000 with Rohit. It paid off. 'Fortunately, we never had to see another day like that again.'

They did not have to because the experience of staring down an empty barrel had taught them the importance of managing cash. They did not want to ever let down their team.

~

Meanwhile, our other hero in the US, Avnish Bajaj, was going through a soft landing in entrepreneurship with Soft Magic. The work convinced him that he wanted to do a business of his own. But he did not plunge headlong into it. After Apple, he wanted to study further in an MBA.

Every school but one rejected him. He wanted to go to Wharton because it was in the San Francisco Bay Area, which had been home for him. But he was wait listed there. Stanford rejected him twice. The university that took him in, magically, happened to be the best of them: Harvard Business School. Then began a journey of transformation and the most enjoyable phase of his life, trumped only by the joy of having children, he would later say.

It is hard for him to pinpoint what exactly it was that he learned at Harvard. All he can say is that it was like getting into a washing machine as Person X and coming out—after the rolling and tumbling by the lectures, exposure, peer effect and a mid-course internship with McKinsey—as Person Y, who was just a little more sorted than the one who had gone in. Person Y also had the seed of entrepreneurship planted in his head all over again—this time more firmly.

It was at Harvard that Avnish met Suvir Sujan, who went on to set up Baazee with him. They did a field project together, sponsored by a professor, to build a company to outsource work from India. They spent a few weeks in India in 1997. The information technology services boom had just begun in the country, and the three met a bunch of companies in the area, some big, some small. It did not take them long to realize that this business was not for them.

IT services out of India in those days was a lot about 'body shopping'—an export of people rather than services to the US. It was more like a glorified visa management business. H1B was a like a lottery, something to wait for with bated breath. It was unsexy, unglamorous and boring.

Avnish's passion, not least because of his stint with Apple, lay in doing things that touched the customer directly. But he was not sure what that passion could be. So he and Suvir, still convinced they had to do something of their own, agreed to stay in touch and see how things would go.

McKinsey, at the end of Avnish's internship, offered him a job, but he turned it down and went to work with Goldman Sachs in New York in the investment bank's high technology practice. The years from 1998 to 2000 saw the dotcom bubble build up. Avnish worked crazy hours, seven days a week. Those were intense days. He worked on many interesting deals. He sat across the table from Michael Eisner as Disney's long-time CEO bought Infoseek. That gave him immense confidence. Then another big deal changed the course of his life.

Avnish was part of the Goldman team that handled the follow-on public offer of eBay, the popular online marketplace. He studied the model and was struck by its novelty. Amazon was very big already, as was Yahoo. But Amazon was an online bookstore. Yahoo was an online newspaper. The other online retailers were in effect offline retailers who had found an outlet online.

eBay, on the other hand, was all new, a product of the Internet. Its concept of a marketplace that defied geographical limitations could not exist without the Internet, while the other businesses could and did thrive before the Internet caught on. At that time, in 1999–2000, the term online marketplace had not even been coined and eBay was already one. It was different, and fascinating.

Suvir, too, was in New York, with the Boston Consulting Group. He and Avnish would often meet to dream of their own business. The business plans they made were, understandably, US-focused. That was where it was all happening. They felt at home in New York. It took them a while to realize the market had moved while they were still making plans. People had raised money and built businesses. They would be late to the party if they joined in there.

Consulting work with a pharmaceutical company took Suvir to Allahabad in 1999. He came back and told Avnish that India was booming. Until then, it had not struck either of them to build a business in India. But the eBay work, which had just got done, made them revisit the idea again.

The more Avnish thought about it, the better it looked. In addition to the business potential, it would help him be closer to his father, who had been diagnosed with Parkinson's in 1994. As his father's health deteriorated, Avnish's parents found it more and more difficult to make their annual visit to their son in New York. His sister was shifting from India to Canada. His parents needed their son in India.

Though Avnish would have loved to call it a bold, well-thought-out move, it was more a coming together of circumstances that brought him back to India. The only thought-through parts were the ideas Avnish and Suvir used to bounce off Scott Murphy, an entrepreneur and consultant. He had become a sort of mentor to them. Finally, Avnish told him they were thinking of moving to India and doing something there.

'How can I help?' Scott asked.

'I have no money,' said Avnish.

What he had, instead, was $100,000 of debt. About half of that was the education loan he had taken for the business school course. He had no savings from his time with Apple. A software engineer in those days made something like $55,000 a year, before tax. And Avnish was living it up. Credit card debts and bank overdrafts had mounted.

'I have no money to buy my plane ticket, no money for a laptop,' he told Scott.

'Let's go for a walk,' said Scott.

They walked. And talked. Before Avnish realized which way they were walking, they had reached Scott's office, near Union Square in New York. Scott opened his cheque book and wrote out one for $20,000 in Avnish's name.

'I trust you,' said Scott. 'You have been talking about these plans, go make it happen. If I lose this money, I will not regret it. If something comes out of it, I'm sure you will be fair to me and give me an appropriate stake.'

There was nothing else discussed. Avnish did not have a business yet, but he already had an angel investor. He booked himself on a flight to India.

Scott Murphy went on to become a member of the US Congress.

~

'You are too ideological. You are too young to be so ideological,' Avnish Bajaj told Yogi. Yogi was trying to control too many things. 'For a marketplace to succeed, it has to be open. Let things come up in their own way.'

By this time, numerous properties were approaching Stayzilla for a listing. Yogi would tell many of them he would get back to them once demand in their city increased. It took time for Yogi to come round to Avnish's view that supply created its own demand. Stayzilla opened up supply by March 2014. Every time supply increased, demand did too. And Yogi was left kicking himself for not doing it earlier. Thankfully, he was the first to market and had the luxury of making mistakes.

In February 2015, Stayzilla raised another round of funding—$20 million—with Nexus coming in and Matrix putting in some more. Some angels exited with fifteen times the money they had put in.

The money made it easier to find talent, one of the trickiest things for start-ups. When I met Yogi, Stayzilla had recently hired fifty-five people from IITs, BITS and the Indian School of Business. It received 2800 applications from IITs. Yogi was 'shocked' at the response.

Stayzilla's Chennai office strength was going to nearly double to 600 by the end of 2015. The Bangalore office was quickly coming to life. The business, Yogi said, would grow five times, with 50,000 properties in 8000 towns by the end of 2015. 'We are not doing anything. Every day, twenty properties list with us on their own. They approach us because we have reached critical mass.'

Half of the business came from tier 3 towns, and a lot from mobile phones. But there was still no app in place when I met Yogi. It was to come later in the year. Stayzilla had done a lot of research before launching its mobile site in April 2014. Many tier-2 and tier-3 towns had poor Internet connectivity. Expecting customers there to download an app would be asking for too much. It could be done now, with the improved connections and speeds.

That is Stayzilla's strength: Yogi likes to think through strategies and plans; he does not act in haste. 'We think a lot. We plan. We never do a one-year plan; we plan for three years.'

That, and the width it has achieved. Other people focus on the obvious holiday hotspots: Delhi, Mumbai, Goa, Agra, Jaipur, Bangalore. Stayzilla would have sizeable capacity in places such as Tirupati, which could generate more room nights than some of the more obvious hotspots. Some of the 'hot cities' listed on its website are Dibrugarh, Munnar, Itanagar, Deoghar, Solapur, Kalka and Guntur.

India is often said to be twenty-nine different countries—that's the number of very diverse states it has. But India can also be looked at as thirty different countries by language and 3000 by caste. Stayzilla has spent nearly a decade understanding this diversity and has chosen to be an end-to-end marketplace for stays, including alternative options like guesthouses, lodges and homestays.

Stayzilla also offers a concierge service, in the manner of five-star hotels. But the Stayzilla concierge works at stays whose owners will struggle to pronounce the word 'concierge'.

Stayzilla's concierge sets you free. It is the bridge and buffer between the stay and the customer. In the run-up to the travel, neither the customer nor the owner/manager of the stay will have to bother with unnecessary calls about the booking. They can route the calls to the concierge, who will work things out and keep both parties informed. In the beginning of a relationship with Stayzilla, its concierge will call the customer every now and then, but much less so for subsequent engagements once Stayzilla gets to know them better.

~

Shashank and Abhinav's first product was Practo Ray, which helped doctors digitize patient data. Expectedly, it was dependent on doctors buying in. It would fail if they did not get on to the platform and would be left with the option of doing precisely what the two failed US companies had tried: make consumers (patients) get on to the platform instead.

The question was, how to get doctors to adopt a software for which they had to pay.

Practo Ray was a SaaS—software as a service—that allowed doctors to manage their schedules, their patients' records and billing—all on one platform. In 2009, SaaS was still a new concept. It promised easier, speedier and cheaper implementation, unlike the old model, which involved licensing, consulting fees, training costs, extra infrastructure, ongoing maintenance fees and cumbersome implementation. SaaS was hosted by the vendor and accessed by the customer over the Internet.

With regular software, one would buy a compact disc with the software loaded in it. Practo Ray, being a SaaS, would charge a subscription fee. It was a lot to ask of doctors, to both understand the concept and to pay for it. Many of them did not understand software very well.

Shashank and Abhinav had to answer tricky questions. 'So this CD is for Rs 5000,' some doctors would say, 'and on top of that you want me to pay Rs 10,000 a year. Why would I pay an annual fee if I have already paid for the CD?'

'But this is the new technology, it works on the Internet,' Shashank or Abhinav would explain, and go on to list its benefits.

'But,' the questions kept coming, 'why will I not prefer something that works offline? For that I will not need an Internet connection and can use it anywhere.'

Shashank and Abhinav would have to explain all they knew about the evolution of technology, how the old CD will vanish and how the Internet was the future.

Only 1 per cent of the doctors they met saw their point. It was a slow process for the two, creating the market that exists today, where doctors are open to buying software and using it. And paying for it.

It was a long journey. Shashank would hit the road on his motorcycle to meet doctors. After the meetings, he would come back to the office to share the product roadmap with Abhinav so he could build the product. The two coded the first version of the product themselves, sharing the work equally. With time, Shashank's share of the coding kept declining as he started to spend more and more time on sales pitches. Then they added sales guys. The team grew to eight, comprising mostly close friends.

They now began to cover three to four cities—Bangalore and adjoining settlements. They would travel by the local trains to sell their software to doctors. Out of the money they earned, they paid themselves meagre salaries. Elsewhere, their friends and college mates were enjoying lavish lifestyles in corporate set-ups.

Shashank feels nothing but amazement when he looks back at what they actually pulled off. Grit and determination kept them going. They had no experience. There was no businessman in Shashank's family. Both his parents worked safe, public sector jobs—the father with the Steel Authority of India and mother with Bharat Electronics Ltd.

By the time they graduated from Surathkal, Shashank and his friend had a product and a few customers. Still, they wondered if they should take up jobs. All their well-wishers were advising them exactly that: 'Work for a few years. You can do your own thing later.'

In hindsight, it appears fortunate that there were not many attractive jobs on offer. Lehman Brothers had fallen, taking down with it the health and sentiment of the global financial markets.

'Go for an MBA,' the well-wishers said, 'like your friends are.'

But Shashank and Abhinav were really enjoying themselves at Practo Ray, even through the sweat and tears of long and tiring days. Shashank loved it when a doctor changed the way he thought about his work and schedule, and his patients benefited. He loved returning to office with the feedback he had collected from his sales pitches to improve the product. 'We felt like creators, [it was] a big high for us.'

The money was low. The odd meal would be missed. But there was a lot to learn every day. Doctors and patients sent constant feedback with the help of a small programme Shashank and Abhinav had made that routed all of it automatically to Practo's website, even the bad feedback.

There were also some nice responses. At times as late as 1 a.m., when Shashank hadn't an ounce of energy left, a doctor would say, 'Look guys, I never believed in software, but your software has changed my clinic, changed me. My patients are so happy. I can't thank you enough.'

That was worth a lot more than a million dollars. Another doctor would simply comment, 'Just to say you guys are doing a great job. Somebody referred your software to me and I bought it, and I am so happy.'

To a bunch of eight young men making the software and selling it in just three or four cities, it was pure joy. They were a close-knit unit, with one car to share among them. The time they were getting Morpheus Venture Partners on board, an advisor called and said he was on his way to Practo's office: He was at such and such place and asked if someone could please go and fetch him. That day the car had already been taken elsewhere, and there were no cabs in sight. So Shashank kick-started his motorcycle, a TVS Apache he had bought in college, and fetched the advisor, who, in his crisp suit and tie, made quite a sight on the pillion seat.

Shashank and Abhinav bootstrapped the business. They put whatever money they had earned back into Practo. They counted every rupee coming in and going out. Sometimes they did not have much to count. Their targets were simple: if you don't earn this money, there will be none to pay salaries. That is the kind of pressure they faced at age twenty-three. It taught them life skills, people skills, and hinted that if they could get through those days, they could get through anything.

They participated in business planning competitions to earn money. The prize money used to be high—Rs 1 lakh to Rs 5 lakh. They did not always win. It was ironic that they had built a real business and were making some money; yet, on occasion they would lose to people whose ideas had remained just ideas.

~

Suchi Mukherjee had her honeymoon two years after her wedding, when she could find the time for it. She wanted to go to a place where mobile phones did not work. The tightest leash that ties you to work in investment banking is the phone. It keeps you on the job all the time. You take calls at dinner, in the gym and in the bathroom. The last thing you do before falling asleep is to check your email. Which is also the first thing you do on waking up.

When Suchi got fifteen days off for her much-delayed honeymoon, she went to Africa. There, for the first time after she began to work in 1998, she had the time to sit back and think. What did she really want to do with her life and career?

She liked banking and thought she was good at it. But she wanted to build something, too—which might not be a bank like Lehman; she would rather be a Lehman client than a Lehman managing director.

In 2003, a year after the honeymoon, she left Lehman for NTL, which is now called Virgin Media. It was the UK's largest cable company—a badly run place that was not exactly loved by its customers. The only reason Suchi joined it was Aizad Hussain, who was earlier a banker with Morgan Stanley.

Bankers are, to put it in a nutshell, generally useless. The only thing they learn, know and do is deal negotiation. They do not build anything, they do not run anything. Hussain had made a successful transition and had become an operational leader at NTL. In fact, he had grown it by swallowing many small cable companies.

He also presented Suchi's best chance to make a transition to operations from banking. Having made the change himself, Hussain was likely to take a chance with another banker. That he did with Suchi, putting her in financial planning at NTL, where she worked until one day, six months later, when he called to ask where she was.

'I'm driving,' she said.

'I need to talk to you,' said Hussain, unperturbed. NTL was consolidating all its assets. It was going to work with just two centres in the UK, instead of thirteen. 'I just fired the guy who was going to do it. Now you run operations.'

At the time of joining, Suchi had told Hussain that one day he must give her a real job. Now was the time. She delivered one of the biggest consolidations in the history of UK's cable industry. She spent time on the floor of the call centres counting staff. She fired a bunch of people and rehired them at different centres.

In February 2005, Suchi had her first child, Myra. Now some of the demands NTL made on her, including the travel between London and Manchester, appeared a bit much. Around this time, she was introduced to Douglas McCallum, eBay's managing director for the UK, who had an unwritten rule that he would hire only consultants and MBAs.

'You have been with culturally crappy organizations,' said Doug. 'Why should I hire you?'

'Don't you need to know the filth to know what you don't want?' Suchi shot back. She got the job, probably the first investment banker to join eBay UK, in January 2006.

There she helped build seller support and customer support. Those were heady days for eBay. It grew from 350,000 customers in the UK to 15 million. For Suchi, though, the bigger high was meeting Niklas Zennström, who had sold Skype to eBay and now continued as its CEO.

Suchi always wanted to build a product, but that could not be done at eBay UK; it could only be done in Silicon Valley. Zennström had heard about both her and her ruthlessness for prioritization.

That matters more than you think. A big business has 100 things bubbling away on the stove at any point in time. There is a lot of value in knowing, say, which two must be addressed immediately and which need to be abandoned. Suchi did not let anything bubble for long. Zennström gave her product design and, eventually, global marketing for Skype. Those were great years.

Suchi had a small daughter and was spending several days every month in Estonia, which she only knew as being somewhere close to Finland. eBay had a big engineering base there. For a year after Skype was sold to eBay, the product pipeline was at a standstill because the two organizational cultures clashed. eBay would send senior leaders to Skype who wouldn't blend in with its culture.

Suchi blended, despite being a non-engineer and a woman—indeed, so well that Michael van Swaaij, who was chairman of Skype, is today an investor in LimeRoad. But she still was dying to run a business.

She got her chance in January 2009, when she was told to take charge at Gumtree, a classifieds advertising site eBay had acquired four years earlier. Gumtree was a distant number three when she took charge of it in January 2009. Two years later it was number one in jobs and consumer listings.

~

Mu Sigma was entirely funded by Dhiraj and Ambiga's money for the first three-and-a-half years, with some friends and family chipping in as angel investors. Ambiga led the life of a single parent during this period, balancing her job and their child. They moved into a small apartment. There were no venture capitalists around to say 'take my money', as there are today.

'I am a little conservative. I still believe one should put in one's own money to start a company. I wouldn't want too much debt. I believe in building profitable companies, not those that have no money, no profit and have infinite valuations based on nothing. I understand the logic behind why people do all the other things they do. But I cannot see myself doing it.'

In the beginning, it was difficult to convince prospects to join Mu Sigma. Most of them did not believe in the concept behind it, certainly not enough to leave their jobs for it. It was even more difficult to get customers to pay for its services. But it happened with time. A senior executive from an insurance company would talk to Dhiraj, listen to him intently, and express amazement at what he heard. But he would be too much of a realist, and the insurance company, like all good insurance companies, too conservative. It wouldn't take the plunge with a nobody. Eventually, a technology company gave Mu Sigma a small project, which made the insurance company braver.

Dhiraj fondly remembers his first dinner with the senior executive at the insurance company. Dhiraj had just had three of his wisdom teeth removed and was on sedatives. His face was swollen and he was unable to speak properly. And now, after weeks of perseverance, the client from the insurance company had finally agreed to talk to Dhiraj. 'He is on the phone.' Ambiga's voice pierced Dhiraj's stupor, and he got up with a start. The voice on the phone was a better antidote to Dhiraj's pain than morphine. 'Can we meet for dinner this evening?' Food, or anything that involved the use of teeth, was furthest from Dhiraj's mind. 'Of course,' he found himself saying.

He went to that dinner with a sponge in his mouth. Forget chewing, his head throbbed when he tried to speak. But it was all worth it.

Much later, the senior executive told Dhiraj he had called him to dinner that evening to say he was reluctant to give Mu Sigma the deal. But he did not have the heart to say that after he saw Dhiraj's swollen face and the obvious pain he was in.

Was he joking? By now they knew each other well. 'I wish I had not removed all three teeth that day. We could have got two more customers, one for each tooth,' says Dhiraj, with a short, sharp laugh.

In 2008, FTV Ventures, sensing an opportunity in Mu Sigma, invested $15 million. The money went to some angels who wanted to exit. Later, Sequoia and General Atlantic came on board with a combined $200 million.

The decision to fund Mu Sigma with their own money in the initial years has kept Dhiraj and Ambiga in a very strong position, with control of 47 per cent of the equity. And now, they are in a position to support other entrepreneurs. They have funded two start-ups by Mu Sigma employees.

'Ownership is what defines a company. If you own less than 10 per cent of the company, it doesn't bring out the real intensity of entrepreneurship,' says Dhiraj.

Dhiraj and Ambiga's position at Mu Sigma is in sharp contrast with that of many other founders at other companies, whose stakes have come down drastically to nudge the single digits. This stronghold helped Ambiga make a smooth transition into the CEO's position in February 2016, but created concern when she and Dhiraj said in May that their marriage was over. Ambiga said it will not affect the company. Dhiraj, however, told the *Economic Times* that Ambiga may not remain the CEO in the long-term.

~

redBus was officially launched in 2006. Much earlier, Phanindra Sama had told his human resources manager at Texas Instruments that he was working on a project to solve the bus ticketing problem; that this would not interfere with his office work, and that he would quit his job if his work at the venture conflicted with his work at TI. The HR manager said there was no problem so long as he was not building the same microchip that he was building at Texas Instruments elsewhere.

Phani quit his job just before the official launch of redBus. Now they needed to raise money. They approached Seedfund, an early stage investor, and asked for Rs 30 lakh, for which they were willing to part with 30 per cent equity.

At that time, Rs 1 lakh was big money for them. And a 30 per cent stake for Rs 30 lakh meant the company was valued at Rs 1 crore, the same amount that could be won on *Kaun Banega Crorepati*. It just sounded right.

Bharati Jacob of Seedfund told them the valuation was all wrong.

She sat them down, heard out their business plan and progress, and made them go through several iterations. This was too much equity for too small an amount. The amount was anyway not enough for what they wanted to do, which was to go pan-India.

The inference from their seventh iteration was that they needed Rs 3 crore just to run the business for a year.

'I will give you a cheque for Rs 3 crore, you give me the same 30 per cent,' said Bharati.

It is something Phani will never forget and be forever grateful for. The year was 2006. The money came in early 2007.

Until then, they had bootstrapped and kept expenses low. When they needed to hire their first employee, they just spread the word around. A friend said: 'Here is a distant cousin of mine. He has done his MCA and is not doing anything.'

This distant cousin came over when the founders were learning Java and the rest of the software. They taught him, too. He turned out to be one of the best software engineers at redBus. And so they grew to six, as two other 'distant cousins' came on board.

The six did everything there was to do. In the morning they coded. As the day wore on and calls came in, they doubled as call centre support. They would take a call about something not working and no sooner would they put the phone down than they would be fixing the problem because they were also the software guys. Later in the day they would step out to distribute pamphlets about redBus and its services.

Those were very tiring days, remembers Phani. 'I would wake up in the morning, take calls, make the round of SEZs at lunch and hand pamphlets to people taking a walk after lunch. Go to bus stand in the evening to distribute pamphlets. Come back by midnight. Repeat the whole thing the next day. There was no difference between weekdays and weekends.'

They were very conscious of the money they spent. Food was often low priority. As software engineers, they had wearied of eating at the nicest eateries. As start-up founders, lunch time would find them at the gates of institutions waiting to hand out pamphlets to post-lunch walkers, putting off their own meal because it made more sense to return to their flat to eat.

However, word spread that these guys were on to something big. Money poured in: Rs 43 crore from three investors in three rounds. The venture capital scene in the country was taking off.

In 2007, the most frequent visitors to its office in Bangalore's Domlur locality were venture capitalists (VCs). One VC took a taxi from his hotel, The Leela, to the redBus office. The moment he mentioned redBus, the driver said: 'Yeah, I know the place.'

'Is redBus that famous?' asked the VC. 'Actually,' the driver said, 'there was another *saab* whom I drove to that office just yesterday.' The first question on the gentleman's lips when he entered the redBus office was: 'Which VC met with you yesterday?'

Phani wondered why other start-ups made such a big deal about raising money. There was so much going around. He would raise money when redBus really needed it. There was no hurry. The company was burning only Rs 7-8 lakh a month. It had Rs 1 crore in the bank, left over from the first round of funding given by Seedfund's Bharati Jacob. Seedfund was one of India's leading early stage VC funds.

Things couldn't have been better. Until Lehman Brothers collapsed on 15 September 2008.

From the next day there would be no VC knocking on the door. And now redBus really needed money.

Its bank balance was down to Rs 60 lakh. It fell further because a loan had to be disbursed to Charan Padmaraju, one of the three co-founders, who needed cash for a family emergency. There was not enough left to see them through more than four months. Even if a VC agreed to give them money, it would take four to five months to reach redBus's bank account. It was time to start working the phones again.

Only, the tables had now turned. VCs would not take their calls. Even those who had come knocking before Lehman fell had changed their tune. 'We are not writing any cheques at the moment.'

Sanjay Anandaram of Seedfund, who was playing mentor to redBus, came to the rescue. 'Kanwal Rekhi is in town for the TiEcon, go meet him. I'll tell him to expect you,' he said.

Rekhi, head of Inventus Capital Partners, was a legend in the world of start-ups. He had invested in several of them, and had also co-founded The Indus Entrepreneurs (TiE), the largest global network of Indian entrepreneurs.

Phani met him at The Lalit in Bangalore. Rekhi liked what Phani told him about redBus. He was also comforted by Anandaram's presence. 'You have network effect,' Rekhi said, approvingly.

Phani was relieved. When he returned home after the meeting, he googled 'network effect'.

Rekhi's interest added to the network effect. Now Helion Venture Partners, another India-focused fund, wanted a piece of redBus. Seedfund was ready to make a pro rata investment to safeguard its stake. The three put in Rs 8 crore, infusing new life into redBus.

But the money came at a cost. This time the valuation was much lower than it had been in the first round of funding. redBus's revenues had grown six times between the two rounds. It had been embraced by the ecosystem of bus operators, agents and travellers. So theoretically, the second round of funding should have happened at a higher valuation per share. But Lehman had changed everything.

Phani rationalized that the lower valuation was the price to be paid because of the timing. Many other start-ups were gasping for funding and not finding it. It was also a time when rivals to redBus had cropped up, but were also slowing down because of lack of capital. Thanks to the Rs 8 crore that had come in now, redBus could make rapid strides.

Only to trip up at home.

The company's senior managers, all of whom owned shares in the company, thought Phani had given up too much equity for too little money. This changed the mood dramatically. From a red-hot start-up, redBus came to be seen as a stepchild reluctantly adopted by investors.

Phani had to find ways to motivate and manage his people. Sudhakar Pasupunuri, his buddy from BITS Pilani and co-founder, wanted to leave. Charan, the third co-founder, understood Phani, but he could not convince the others that Phani had done the right thing.

Phani already had his hands full. His parents wanted him to find a wife and settle down. There had been no time for love and courtship over the last few years. And his stock was not exactly soaring in the arranged marriage market. Fathers of prospective brides did not see much of a future for their daughters with Phani. One of the wiser ones enquired, 'Doesn't he sell private bus tickets?'

There was not much time for rebuttal even if Phani wanted to launch into one. He was too busy to make frequent trips to Nizamabad, where his parents lived and where the battle lines for his arranged marriage were being drawn.

Given a choice, Phani too may have considered leaving, just like Sudhakar. But what would he resign from? Whom would he leave? Whom would he be escaping from ? This was where he belonged.

Phani, Charan and Sudhakar had not acquired any trappings of wealth. Probably because they did not have any. They drew survival salaries at redBus. Phani rode a 100 cc motorcycle. 'Maybe you should not have given up the Texas Instruments job,' his parents said.

That was it.

'I want a break for ten days,' he found himself telling his board of directors. He had stumbled on this vipassana thing while surfing the Net, and it seemed like the perfect place to slow his mind down. He had not been away from work even for a day since starting redBus, unofficially, in 2005. Surprisingly, the board said, 'Go for it.'

And Phani found himself at the vipassana centre, feeling very much troubled by thoughts of what could be going on back in the real world.

Now, sitting in front of the instructor, he found himself saying, 'I have serious matters back home.'

'That you had before you came,' said the instructor. 'You put considerable thought into the decision to come here.' The instructor sounded just like Phani's own inner voice. 'Give it a shot, you won't regret it.'

Somewhere inside Phani the two voices converged, and he stayed on.

～

CHAPTER 5

Phani came back from the vipassana a changed man. The session had calmed him down. No one had resigned at redBus while he was away. Nothing had changed. It was an epiphany for him that the company would not collapse without him it might not collapse at all. They had a good thing going. He also thought increasingly more about the Tata Group.

He was struggling to run one company, how did Ratan Tata run 100? How did he manage the stress? One day, he saw a quarter page ad in the *Economic Times*. It had J.R.D Tata's face on it and a quote from him saying: 'If I have any merit, it is getting along with individuals according to their ways and characteristics. At times it involves suppressing yourself. It is painful, but necessary. To be a leader you have to lead human beings with affection.'

The quote had all the answers Phani was seeking: 'It is painful but you have to do it.'

He cut out the ad, framed it, hung it in his office, and named the largest conference room in the redBus office the JRD Room. He had found the management principle by which to run his company. He was no longer impatient for results. He would sit back and let other people do their job. Of course at times there would be chaos, Phani would only ensure that the chaos was creative.

He was not rattled even when Sudhakar finally left, saying, 'This time, don't stop me. I have stopped enjoying this.' He was always the most thoughtful of the three.

The third round of funding happened in 2011. They didn't really need the money, but, singed from the scarcity that had occurred overnight before the second round, Phani chose to play it safe. Better take the money when people are offering it, he told himself, instead of having to go begging for it later.

They did not know how much to raise. But Rs 30 crore had a nice ring to it, since Rs 30 lakh was what they were looking for the first time they went out to raise money. They put the money in the bank. redBus was now profitable.

In many ways, 2012 was a boom year in Indian e-commerce funding. Flipkart and Snapdeal were raising big money. Finally, investors had begun to believe in India's e-commerce story. The knocks on redBus's door had become more frequent, and louder. The company was not really looking for money. But a fairly large VC wanted to check if one of the existing investors would sell their shares.

Seedfund, the first investor, had spent nearly six years in redBus. The particular fund within Seedfund from which that money had come was drawing to a close. And the offer from this large VC was really good. The redBus founders pricked up their ears: it was best to talk to everybody and choose the new investors, they thought.

There were three VCs invested in redBus, and then there was the fourth lot of shares with the three co-founders. So there were four parties holding the entire redBus equity. They decided to call in an investment banker, Avendus, to talk to all four, and also to potential investors.

By this time, the new investors were playing for higher stakes. 'We run a large fund,' said one of them. 'We will invest at least $30 million if we invest at all.'

'The more the merrier,' said the co-founders.

At this time, Ibibo, the world's largest online travel company, made them an offer that was impossible to refuse. They did not want to merely invest, they wanted to buy the whole company.

Now the game had changed. But the window for such a deal was very small. redBus was already in advanced stages of signing a deal with a VC. That window caused a crack because there was a death in the family that kept the head of the VC away for a week.

'You have a week,' the promoters told Ibibo.

'That's sufficient, we will close the deal,' said Ibibo, and flew in its lawyers. The Ibibo lawyers locked themselves up in a room with the redBus lawyers and emerged after a week with the deal in hand. There was hardly any due diligence done, and $135 million was changing hands. The deal was finalized in June 2013.

Among the senior management, only Phani, the CEO, and Bharat Singh, the CFO, knew about it. Charan, the CTO, found out after it had been finalized. He had to be told a couple of days before the deal was announced because he had to sign some documents as a shareholder.

The rest of the team was told about it in July 2013. In August, Phani took his family to London. He was now married, and he and wife, Sarika, had become proud parents of a little girl. They had never really had much of a honeymoon. Phani's parents had never been abroad. He would remain the redBus CEO for another year, but this holiday was well-earned.

He still retained the lessons from the vipassana. Nothing would go wrong if he were to go away for a few days.

But by the time he came back, everything had. Phani was no longer the nicest man in the world of Indian start-ups. To

Ibibo, he was the man who did a deal, took their money, and disappeared. To his team, he was a slimy bastard.

∼

By early 2010, some of the merchants with Jasper, Kunal and Rohit's company, told them that many online companies were reaching out to them to list their coupons online. Kunal and Rohit said they could do it, too.

On Republic Day, the two spent eight hours in Costa Coffee at Rajouri Garden in west Delhi, a short walk from their office, and came up with a name and plan for the online business, even though it was still not much of a plan at the time. Other than registering a domain name, they did not know much about running an Internet business. But youth has its own ways. They were confident about pulling it off.

Eight days later, Snapdeal was up on the Internet. It was not much to begin with, really. A large number of transactions failed. Nevertheless, it was a deal site on the Internet. The merchants who were in Jasper's coupon book had gone online. So the supply side did not change much, but it was on the web, which was no small change.

Interestingly, Snapdeal was not the first deal site. It was the seventh. Within six months, there were fifty more. But Snapdeal, with its large supply base of merchants, scaled up the fastest, leaving behind the likes of Smile Group's DealsandYou.

The others were focused more on generating demand. Snapdeal created so much supply that demand came on its own. Within fourteen months of its launch, it had a 70 per cent share of the market. The investor community thought it was running away with the coupon space. So funding followed, from a bunch of pedigreed investors like Kaalari Capital,

Indo US Ventures and Nexus. Snapdeal raised $10 million. That may sound modest in today's day and age, when $100 million in funding has become commonplace. But it was a big milestone back in 2011, when funds were drying up for Internet ventures.

The investors were, however, in for a surprise. In the middle of 2011, as Snapdeal lorded it over the online deals market, many of its merchants came to Kunal and Rohit once again. This time they said they wanted to sell physical products online, not just deals. And consumers too were saying that they wanted to buy products online.

Kunal and Rohit could have ignored the feedback from their suppliers and buyers. They could have said, 'We are in services, why should we do products?' Or they could follow the natural demand and supply that was knocking at its doors.

They decided to go the natural way.

They started listing some products on Snapdeal, which did well. The turning point was when they went to China in 2011 and saw Alibaba and the vibrant online commerce it was conducting in the country. They realized how big product e-commerce could become in India. But first Snapdeal would have to change its character.

Most of the online commerce in India was done by retailers who would pre-buy products, list them on their website, and then wait for buyers—which was not serving a real need. And serving a real need is the only way to build a large, sustainable business.

The real need was to provide the fragmented, long-tail of supply in India the ability to supply locally but sell nationally. Many merchants and companies had great products but no distribution. Ninety-three per cent of retail in India was unorganized. Organized retail, now at 7 per cent, had little hope of expanding because real estate costs as a percentage of retail sales in India was fourteen times that in the US. The solution had to be one that did not involve real estate cost.

Snapdeal started signing up sellers. Kunal and Rohit told them that if they could create a large supply and attach it to this thick demand pipe Snapdeal had generated for its deals business, transactions would definitely grow. The same consumer, instead of looking for deals, would buy a phone, watch or clothing. But by this time, the online deals business had begun to lose steam.

Spare a thought for their investors, who had given them another $40 million in July 2011, to make it an even $50 million, all of it predicated on the deals business thinking they were investing in the runaway leader in the online deals market.

Just a few months later, in December, Kunal and Rohit were told investors that Snapdeal was shutting down the deals business to do something completely different—to become an online marketplace for businesses, which no one in India had done thus far. There was eBay, but it was an open marketplace, allowing everyone including individuals to sell on its platform, and it also carried used goods. It had an infinite selection and a great range of products (assortment or selection), but the customer experience was not always great. The seller shipped directly to the buyer and eBay had no control over that leg of the process.

At the other end of the spectrum was the inventory-led model, in which the e-commerce company kept stocks of goods sold on its platform. It provided for a lot of control over the quality of goods and the user experience. But it did not have great economics. An e-retailer who follows the inventory-led model needs to have at least 20,000 products in the warehouse if it displays 10,000 on its site. Keeping inventory is expensive, and unsold inventory even more so.

No one was doing the Alibaba-type of managed marketplace, one that would have space only for screened businesses, and would control quality, control user experience and carry only new, unused products. The Alibaba model provided a happy combination of the enormous assortment of a third-party marketplace and high quality as well as user experience of an inventory-led model.

Thus, in January 2012, Kunal and Rohit declared that Snapdeal would be an online marketplace for products. It would have no need for inventory. It would be a platform to bring together sellers (mostly small and medium businesses) and buyers (individual consumers).

'Everyone thought we had gone mad,' says Kunal. Still, the investors supported the founders' decision, albeit with some cautionary advice. The cautionary note was understandable. This was déjà vu all over again. First, Kunal and Rohit thought coupons was going to be a billion-dollar business. Then they thought online deals would truly be big. However, there were just not enough restaurants, spas and salons in India and just not enough people patronizing them. That business would probably never be large enough to justify the $50 million Jasper had raised. And it would probably never be able to satiate Kunal and Rohit's ambition, which was to solve a real, large problem.

The online marketplace could do both. So they began to build supply all over again, as aggressively as ever. They had done it before. This time, though, they were talking to different businesses. These were small chaps selling products, not services.

Today, all of Snapdeal's business consists of products, and the company is now valued at billions of dollars.

The online marketplace is all the rage now. At the time Snapdeal became one, Flipkart, the largest and most valued of the e-commerce companies, was purely inventory-led. It bought goods to sell on its site, and did not allow others to set up shop. It was only in 2013 as Amazon, the world's largest electronics retailer and an open marketplace, entered India that Flipkart began to offer up its site as a marketplace as well.

~

Back in India, Avnish Bajaj was still not sure what he was going to do. There was a bunch of ideas. Rediff was one of the early stars among the Indian start-ups, doing news and also a bit of e-commerce. Avnish and Suvir toyed with the idea of building a bigger, better Rediff. They thought of city-specific portals, but soon gave up on the idea. And, of course, they thought of an e-Bay-like venture.

Around this time they had come to know Ashish Dhawan, who was a year senior to them at Harvard Business School. He returned to India to start ChrysCapital, a venture capital firm. Somehow they managed to keep their friendship distinct from their brewing relationship as potential entrepreneurs and investor. At times, all three would sleep over in the same apartment and make their way to Dhawan's office in the morning, to sit across the table and negotiate with each other. Eventually ChrysCapital agreed to put in $1.2 million.

One night at his parents' home in Delhi, Avnish was browsing through a Hindi–English dictionary looking for a name for his company. Just before dawn, around 3.30 a.m., he woke Suvir up with a call.

'I have the perfect name,' Avnish said. '*Baazi.*' It was Hindi for bet.

Suvir found it interesting, but preferred to spell it as 'Baazee'. Just like that, the christening was done.

After ChrysCap, they found more investors to bet on them. Baazee was moving fast. There was a buzz around it. Avnish and Suvir were looked upon as contrarians—those were still the days of the brain drain—who were running against the stream by quitting high-paying jobs in the US to come back home.

At that time the average entrepreneur in India was in his forties, from old-world businesses. Avnish and Suvir were in their twenties, trying to make something work on the Internet. They were the 'brain gain' guys, and got a lot of good press. Funds began to flow in, including a large chunk from Rupert Murdoch. In all they raised $21 million even before the Baazee website was launched.

It may never have been launched had they done their due diligence. India had abysmal Internet and computer penetration. It was probably the only major country that saw a decline in Internet users between 2000 and 2002.

In 2000, the term 'dotcom' was so fashionable the joke was that adding .com to your name would get you a salary hike. Several venture-funded Internet service providers were giving away Internet connections for free in the hope that advertising would be followed by subscribers. Then the bubble burst. Funding dried up. Some ISPs went bust or sold their businesses to bigger companies.

Free Internet access disappeared. Baazee hit a brick wall. Its founders went back to the drawing board. 'Do we believe in the core of this model: a peer-to-peer marketplace and exchange?' they asked themselves.

The answer was a resounding yes. Not based on opinion, but on data—data on transactions in the online marketplace, data on how people were rating one another, data on how those transacting included people from Jhumri Telaiya to Mumbai.

Clearly, there was nothing wrong with the core of the model. The problem was with Internet usage; there just was not enough of it in the country and it would be a challenge to scale it up. So the founders decided to 'stick to the core'.

All around them, several online companies were starting to go offline. Baazee wouldn't do that, but it needed to build adjunct businesses to open up other revenue streams so it could survive till the market picked up again.

It built two adjunct businesses, both of which were technology-based and business-to-business. B2B, unlike a B2C, or business-to-consumer business, did not depend on large sections of the population having access to the Internet. It only needed connectivity among its business users, which was in place.

One of the adjunct businesses was a reverse auction engine for procurement. In a reverse auction, several sellers offer their items and compete for the price the seller will accept. It worked for Baazee. All the seats in the INOX theatres in Mumbai and Pune, for instance, were sold through its reverse auction system. It did solidify procurement. It worked with Standard Chartered Bank for paper procurement.

The second revenue stream it opened was auctioning of cars repossessed by lenders. This was the time when a large number of people, thanks to the slowing economy, were not able to pay the EMIs on their cars. Baazee tied up with several banks, including ICICI, which became its biggest client. The cars the banks had taken away from their defaulting borrowers were put up by Baazee on its platform and auctioned to dealers. Baazee also provided Internet access to dealers for this.

These businesses did not change Baazee's core as they were mere extensions of it. At the same time, they helped it tide over what was a very, very difficult period.

In the two-and-a-half years leading up to mid-2003, so many online outfits went belly up that dotcom came to be ridiculed as 'dotcon'.

'People made fun of you. At times it was embarrassing to present your business card,' says Avnish.

Several of his Harvard classmates found themselves out of work as careers were destroyed globally. Baazee was under a lot of pressure, too. Often, before its board meetings, Avnish would tell Tina, who was then his girlfriend, that he did not know if he would still have a job by the time the board meeting ended. He was only half joking.

Apart from the new revenue streams, what pulled the company through was its work culture, which was not built consciously. In fact, it was only years later that the founders realized how close-knit the team was, and remains to this day. The core team consisted of the five members in the executive management team. They were like family. Over drinks, they would tell each other how much the world sucked, but that they were in it together, and that no one was going to give up. That if they went down, they would all go down as one.

This spirit percolated down from the executive management team to the middle management, and trickled down further to engulf the entire 100-strong staff. If one looks at the 'regrettable attrition'—the resignation of those whom one really wants to keep—it would have been less than 10 per cent during the four-and-a-half years that Baazee was owned and run by Avnish and Suvir.

They still have Baazee reunions. When Avnish and I spoke, in March 2015, there had been a reunion three weeks earlier. Fifty-five people came for it, from Germany, Thailand, Australia, Switzerland and from all over India. They have gone on to work at many places, but they say they have never seen a work culture similar to the one they enjoyed at Baazee.

The team spirit saw them through the dotcom bust. That, and the money they had raised before the market went down.

At the end of 2002, there was another company in the same space as Baazee: Bidorbuy. The entire online market was becoming divided between the two. Avnish admits that Bidorbuy had the better platform. But Baazee had the money. At the end of 2002, it acquired Bidorbuy.

The timing was perfect. The environment and market for dotcoms began to improve from the middle of 2003. The India Shining campaign, though it did nothing for its creator, the Bharatiya Janata Party, in the 2004 Parliament elections, did perk up popular sentiment. Baazee, the undisputed leader in its segment, now armed with Bidorbuy's technology and team, surged ahead.

It was at the end of 2003 that Avnish met Meg Whitman, who ran eBay. It was meant to be an introductory meeting, nothing more. So he was surprised when, a few months later, in early 2004, eBay got in touch with an intent to invest in Baazee. Soon that turned into a desire for control.

~

In December 2010, Vijay Shekhar Sharma had to shelve an initial public offering of One97 Communications that was meant to raise Rs 120 crore from the public.

It had seemed a very good idea. The company's revenues and profit before tax, interest and depreciation had grown twenty-fold since SAIF Partners had invested in it in 2007. However, by December 2010, when the IPO was about to open, the stock market went into turmoil as a housing scam broke and the global markets became choppy. Shares of companies that had recently raised money from the public were trading below the prices at which they were issued.

Vijay's merchant bankers said the issue price of his shares had to be brought down sharply to get any subscription. He said he would rather postpone the IPO.

'We were not really desperate for money. We were generating cash and profits.'

By August next year, with the market staying uncertain, the postponement turned into a withdrawal. It is something Vijay is glad for. 'Had we gone public, we would not have been able to do what we are doing now.'

A publicly held company has many masters. It has to be accountable for its decisions to a large number of shareholders.

That is good for transparency and keeps a company focused on what works for it. But it also confines the company to the straight and narrow, prevents it from making ambitious bets, and reduces chances of exponential growth and expansion.

At the time of the IPO, Vijay's ideas were based on what were called feature phones, or instruments that were good for voice calls and SMS but little else. But smartphones, enabling the use of the Internet and all kinds of applications, were already gaining ground. As One97 had morphed from a mobile messaging company into a content and mobile commerce company, smartphones were going to be its best friends. In 2010, spectrum for third-generation mobile telephony (3G) had been auctioned. The new service, with its promise of faster Internet speed, started in the country the following year.

Vijay had hired Abhishek Rajan, a junior from the Delhi College of Engineering, in April 2009. It was Abhishek's responsibility to develop the company's commerce business vertical. In June, Abhishek suggested the name, Paytm, short for pay through mobile, which Vijay liked instantly. In November, Paytm Mobile Solutions was registered as a subsidiary of One97. The first version of its prepaid recharge website—paytmonline.com—was launched in August 2010.

In the first week, Paytm used to get less than forty recharge transactions a day, amounting to Rs 5000 or so. Traffic increased as the company started giving a month's free subscription to its SMS jokes package. Four months later, the company got the domain name paytm.com. By that time it was doing Rs 1 lakh worth of recharges a day—a twenty-fold growth without a penny spent on marketing and promotion. This grew quickly to Rs 50 lakh a day in another year or so as smartphones became more and more popular.

But Vijay was itching to do more. He had to break out of the shackles of the mobile operator's wallet. So far, most of his revenue came as a share of the revenue the operator earned, or was in some way linked to it. He had seen in the US how smartphones had played a role in the spread of consumer Internet. He had to create something that would not be hitched to the operator's wallet.

To create a new wallet, you need to identify a consumer need. To identify a consumer need, you need to identify a problem. Paytm had already branched out into utility payments. Users could pay their electricity bills, DTH charges, etc., through Paytm now.

These were crucial services, but confined by their categories. The biggest problem in India is—as it was then—that a large percentage of its population is not part of the banking system. This is a problem and a need, underlined by the government's *Jan Dhan* programme to open bank accounts.

In 2012, Paytm applied to the Reserve Bank of India for a licence to start an electronic wallet in which users could store money and use it to make payments. The licence came at the end of 2013. The Paytm wallet started in January 2014. In just a year, 20 million people had taken to it, the number rising to 100 million in the middle of 2015, by which time transactions had crossed 75 million a month.

This rapid growth could be attributed to the digital wallet fulfilling a need. Many people are not comfortable with cash. Credit and debit card penetration is very low in India. Even if you have a card, the person whom you have to pay may not be in a position to receive payments through your card or through Internet banking. For small payments of Rs 100 to Rs 300, it seemed cumbersome to use a card or punch in a lot of numbers or a one-time password into a mobile phone. Some users were plain wary of exposing their entire bank account by using their debit cards.

The digital wallet on the mobile has stepped in to fill this gap and is making O2O possible—which is jargon for online-to-offline or offline-to-online—bringing offline commerce and trade online and vice versa.

If you have a mobile phone, all you need to do is to register your number on Paytm or any other digital wallet provider. You receive a one-time password. Enter it and you have a wallet. Paytm verifies the mobile number. No paperwork needs to be done if you spend under Rs 10,000 a month. You need to furnish other documents if you wish to transact for higher amounts.

Paytm says its wallet can be used with 15,000 online merchants, including big ones such as MakeMyTrip, HealthKart, HomeShop18, Uber, eBay, Jabong and Groupon. Then there are the platforms that give access to offline services, such as food, taxi, spa, carpentry and plumbing services. You could buy from Foodpanda, Domino's Pizza, TinyOwl, Swiggy, UrbanClap, Tooler and so on, using the Internet wallet.

In July 2015, Paytm made a breakthrough, getting companies to use its wallet to make direct payments. One of them is NoBroker. As the name suggests, its mobile app and website promises to do away with the broker in renting homes. It brings together the owner and the potential tenant, leaving it to them to take the deal ahead. No fee is charged, and it strictly keeps out the property broker, who would typically take a month's rent each from both owner and tenant, earning a steep commission of 17 per cent.

If you list a property on NoBroker's website or app, you will get a small reward. To receive it, all you have to do is to furnish your Paytm wallet number.

'We know we will change the lives of the half-a-billion people who have no access to banking,' says Vijay.

In the middle of 2014, Paytm started its online marketplace just like Snapdeal and ShopClues, but it was driven mainly by the mobile app. Initially, it was like monetizing its recharge and wallet customers by inducing them to buy on the marketplace. Soon, however, the marketplace grew bigger and began to channel its customers towards the other services, such as wallet, recharge, utility payments and travel tickets.

~

Suchi Mukherjee had her second child, a boy she named Adit, in the summer of 2010. During her maternity leave, she began to think about the future. This time it was not just about her career. Another question began to gnaw at her mind: where did she want her children to grow up? Her parents had given her a strong sense of identity. How would she make sure she gave her children one too?

To her, Delhi was home. That had never been in doubt, even during the seventeen years she had lived in England. She was just an Indian building things there, living a particular experience. Her husband, Sandeep, too, had always thought of himself as an Indian from Delhi. Their children, growing up in England, did not quite know what they were: Indian, Asian British, or what?

One day, soon after Adit was born, Suchi was flipping through a magazine and saw a beautiful pair of earrings. She felt like touching them, and maybe buying them too. They were from a store in Mumbai. She told Sandeep about it in the evening, telling him how bad she had felt that the earrings she liked so much were inaccessible to her.

As she kept ruminating over this, two things became clear to her. First, there wasn't an outfit out there that made the discovery of lovely products easy and entertaining, like flipping through a magazine or a photo album. Second, there was no simple and easy way for her to buy many of the lovely things being made in many parts of Asia.

She started spending time on Amazon, Flipkart, Myntra, Yebhi, Jabong and the other consumer Internet platforms. But she did not enjoy the browsing experience at any. That was when she started discussing with a bunch of friends the possibility of doing something out of India. She got introduced to four investors, two of whom eventually put money into LimeRoad.

Suchi was still on maternity leave from Gumtree when she began to make visits to India, looking at small, interesting companies in the consumer Internet space that she could help scale up. But there was nothing compelling.

She was clear she would not do just retail. Consumer Internet is not about just being a retailer with a website on which one could buy and sell. That was no fun.

Suchi liked social platforms; eBay, Skype and Gumtree were all social platforms. Users did more on them than merely transact. They contributed to the platforms. eBay had made millionaires out of sellers. Skype was all about connecting people. Gumtree had user-generated content.

Suchi's own magic moments had been on social platforms. Myra was a year-and-a-half when, one day, her nanny told Suchi at 10 p.m. that she had go away for a few days because her brother had died. Suchi had a big presentation to make the next day.

She posted an ad on Gumtree at 11.30 p.m. and went to sleep. At 5 a.m., when she opened her computer, she found fifty-two applications. By 10 a.m. she had sorted the applications, referenced the shortlisted ones and hired a temporary nanny—all on the platform she had built.

On another occasion, when she was moving home, she found she had no place in the new house for a beautiful teak chest of drawers she owned. The movers were arriving at 10 a.m. the next day. She posted an ad to sell the piece of furniture at half past midnight on Gumtree. Seven minutes later a corporate lawyer responded, saying he was awake and they could talk. Suchi called him. The lawyer was getting married and said he would love to have the chest. He had it picked up from her home before the movers arrived.

Skype would often be bursting with traffic, what with the number of users who could log on at the same time. But memorable was the day when two users wrote to say they had first met on Skype and were now married. Or the day one woman said Skype was the only way she could connect with her children during her long travels.

Magic moments are far more numerous and frequent for Suchi now at LimeRoad, not least because it is her own venture, which she set up after moving back to India in 2012 with her family. LimeRoad is a social commerce platform for fashion retail online.

'Fashion retail' is a misnomer in India. It is merely a sale of clothes, shoes and accessories. What online retailers sell in the country would be more familiar in Ajmal Khan Road, New Delhi, than Fifth Avenue, New York. This was the business area that saw the first flush of Internet entrepreneurship in India, and the earliest casualties.

Yebhi.com burned down, and is trying to make a comeback in a different avatar. FashionAndYou went sharply up and sharply down, and is trying to claw its way back. Myntra got sold to Flipkart and has struggled with its approach to mobile apps and websites; its founder recently walked out of Flipkart. Jabong, which became popular from its television commercials showing excitable people screaming, is muted these days, and raised funds recently at a much lower valuation than its previous round. Some sites found ways to be at the top of Internet searches, but couldn't sustain it. Some spent their way to the top, through discounts and marketing, and plummeted whenever money became scarce.

Yet, newer ones continue to come in: Koovs, AJIO, Voonik, KharaKapas, Jaypore, StalkBuyLove, ABOF . . . The stream remains as healthy as ever. There are two reasons for that.

The first is high potential. Fashion retail is a $70 billion business in India, of which only 1.5 per cent to 3 per cent is online. This percentage, 15 per cent and more in developed markets, is destined to rise. The second is the high profit margin.

But the time has probably come for everyone to admit that the road to realizing that potential is not straightforward. If it were, the large e-commerce gorillas would have already got there. The biggest among those in the world have not really cracked fashion.

The focused verticals have. That's why Vipshop, a flash sale website listed on the New York Stock Exchange, is the highest valued Chinese e-commerce stock, ahead of Alibaba, a horizontal outfit. Many in England see ASOS as the epitome of all that is good about e-commerce. Some day India may have its own Vipshop or ASOS.

Mukherjee fancies her chances because of the high engagement LimeRoad has come to get from its users. Its website is all about users creating their own look, called a scrapbook. They spend an age matching clothes, shoes, earrings, handbags, watches and so on. The scrapbook makers earn as other users buy the looks they create.

In April 2014, the LimeRoad community was posting 500 units of creatives every day. By December, they were posting 65,000. In the middle of January 2015, when I first met Suchi, this number had increased to 100,000.

'It is a magical moment when you wake up one morning and you look at this thing and you wonder how it became so big.'

The magic goes beyond numbers. There is a schoolteacher in Delhi who was wondering what to do with her life when she retired at sixty, now that her husband had also passed away. She was introduced to LimeRoad by her daughter. She uses its scrapbooks and creates looks with vigour.

Suchi once spoke to a woman in Jharkhand who had created hundreds of looks on the site. This woman wanted to be a designer but knew she could not become one. So she was living her dream on LimeRoad. 'I would love to meet you. We are visiting Patna for a press conference. Will you come?' Suchi asked.

But the woman said her mother would not let her attend the meet.

When I met Suchi again in May 2016, LimeRoad was claiming that 13.5 per cent of its repeat users end up buying something, as do 7.5 per cent of new users. These are very high figures for this segment.

The stuff comes from a network of sellers, while LimeRoad works as a marketplace and focuses on technology. There is untapped potential here. The country has 20 million micro-, small- and medium-sellers of apparel and footwear. Barely 50,000 are online. A platform that brings them together and so close to the buyer can clinch the game, since there is no one dominant player.

'Great products are built out of great connection with people. We are a self-expression platform. Why did Twitter become Twitter and Facebook, Facebook? They are self-expression platforms,' says Suchi.

Suchi, whose LimeRoad stands for self-expression, had found herself at a loss for words when, soon after coming back to India, she sought out a chartered accountant for help in setting up a company.

~

Whatever else one might say, the contractor who ran away with the ShopClues founders' money was not wrong in identifying their stereotype. There is something incongruous about a bunch of NRIs concerning themselves with 300 rupee white shirts.

'We are all about busting stereotypes,' says Radhika. 'That is the goal . . . it is about identifying the customer.'

But how did they deal with the small merchants who were to be brought online? I mean, Radhika still thinks of California more as a home than Gurgaon. How did they take the rough and tumble?

With difficulty, it turns out. In the early days, they would split up and visit different merchants. Sometimes they tried to make these visits fun family outings. The only problem was, Radhika's older son had a problem with strong smells, and he would throw up.

Once, Sandeep and Sanjay went to meet a man called Babbar who sold automotive parts in Karol Bagh. 'Come at noon,' he had said on the phone. 'After that I have to go to an astrology class.'

The two NRIs landed up at this shop sharp on time, but there was no Babbar to be found. They sat down on the pavement right outside his shop in the narrow lane and waited. He turned up eventually, at 2.30 p.m., and did not seem to feel the need for much apology.

The founders were also the merchant acquisition team. They would visit the shops and dealers and say, 'Hey, why don't you sell this stuff online?' Incredulity marked much of the early reaction. The merchants were not sure what was coming next, but became interested when they realized they did not have to do or spend much to do what they were being asked to.

There was no listing fee, no other fee, and a merchant had to pay ShopClues a small fee only when his product was sold. The NRIs took photos of their products and went away. After a while, the merchants would magically get orders for some of the things that had been photographed.

That got them interested, and they began to see how their products were listed and catalogued. An item moved out of their store only when an order was placed for it. Then it moved to a ShopClues' 'fulfilment centre', the kind all online marketplaces have. There it would get inspected, packaged and picked up by a courier. All of it would be done in less than eight hours. The parcel was often couriered through India Post, since ShopClues wanted to reach tier-2 and tier-3 towns.

You can understand the ecstasy with which the ShopClues founders reacted to the first real sale on their website. It had gone up as a Facebook page at the end of 2011. But that restricted access. One had to like the page and obtain an access key to enter the site. The site was thrown open to everyone early in 2012. The first purchase—a coffee mug ordered by a bhadralok in Kolkata—was executed on 14 January 2012. This was the first time someone had placed an order without being prodded.

All three families, with the children, turned up at the fulfilment centre to dispatch the coffee mug to Kolkata. They put a handwritten card into the package with the coffee mug that said: 'Thank you.' It was signed by all the founders.

Shipping was tricky in the early days. A mobile phone would go out and if the buyer was not at the given address, it would come back. The package that came back would be the exact same weight that went out. However, when opened, a little stone elephant, or some such thing weighing exactly the same as the mobile phone, would pop out. One had to admire the expertise of the fellows who did it, if not their integrity.

The relationships with all the early vendors and business partners were handled by the founders. When their office was still being done up, they made Galaxy Hotel in Gurgaon their place of work. Several days a month, one or another of the founders—all of them on certain days—would be seen at the hotel.

'I am really fascinated, overwhelmed, and surprised we managed to do all this.'

Slowly, one coffee mug became several, then several other items; then several other categories, such as auto parts and accessories, kitchen and home appliances, began to move. Interestingly, the early automotive accessories to find a lot of demand were biking gloves and balaclavas.

Word got around that these guys were up to something exciting. They raised $4 million in Series A, in March 2012, when Nexus Venture came in as an early investor. They raised another round, Series B, of $5 million in early 2013, when Helion came in and Nexus made a pro rata investment to preserve its equity percentage.

It seemed nothing could hobble them now.

Then Sandeep got arrested.

~

CHAPTER 6

For a moment, Yogi imagined himself suspended in the air, looking down at himself. What he saw horrified him. He was clad in shorts and banyan, and he was coughing. He was using the breaths between coughs to puff on a cigar.

Stayzilla had been in the market to raise funds—Series A, the first big round from investors—from December 2012. That meant crazy days till August, till the deal was sealed. In the interim, Yogi missed every family milestone: Dad's birthday, mom's birthday, their wedding anniversary, his own wedding anniversary, wife Rupal's birthday, their children's birthdays. Each time, he was somewhere else.

As the funding round closed and Diwali came around, Yogi vowed to spend the festival with family.

By that time he had been smoking for sixteen years. Some time ago, he did a count, and found himself going through two-and-a-half packets a day. So he shifted to the cigar. He thought he was being clever, that the shift to cigar, intense and strong that it was, would cut down his desire to smoke. It may have, in the beginning. He started with five cigars a day, but by October found himself smoking fifteen.

A day before Diwali, he fell ill. He had high fever and a very bad cough. When he woke up on Diwali morning, his entire body ached. He lay in bed coughing. At 5 p.m. that

evening, as the entire neighbourhood was preparing to light
lamps and candles, Yogi dragged himself out of the bed, out
of the house, and to the street corner, where he lit a cigar.
Suddenly, he imagined himself floating up in the air. Then he
looked own and wondered: 'How is this guy I am looking at
ever going to build a billion-dollar company?'

It was not about the money, it was about taking charge
of your destiny, and yourself. The Series A money was in the
bank. But the one day he had planned to celebrate with his
family was completely ruined.

'How pathetic can I get? How can I let smoking control
me?'

He threw the cigar down and came back to the house, to
his room, and to his sick bed. This time he did not lie in the
bed pitying himself. This time he opened his laptop and began
researching.

'How to quit smoking' were the first keywords he googled.
As the Diwali lamps were lit outside and firecrackers rent the
air, Yogi stayed with his laptop, researching ways to quit
smoking. He researched non-stop for twenty-four hours. And
continued reading on the subject for the next month.

He vowed never to smoke—for the sake of his family,
himself, and Stayzilla.

But the smoking addiction, he learned through google, is
not just physiological but also psychological. In a few days
the body stops craving nicotine, but the mind wants the
actions, the imagery: holding the stick between your fingers,
the movement of the hand to the mouth and back, the little
pauses in your speech as you puff on a cigarette, alternating
sips of coffee with puffs on a cigarette. Giving up cigarette is
also about fighting its many associations, which can be done
by creating new associations.

Yogi fought his addiction with his mind and body.
Among other things, he carried a soft, yellow ball everywhere
he went. He played with it, squeezed it, tossed it.

Gradually, the association transformation happened. He has not smoked since that Diwali day in 2013.

Before that, he was almost never seen without a cigarette—during office meetings, investor meetings and most other occasions, it was always a cup of coffee in one hand and a cigarette in the other for Yogi.

Suddenly, the cigarette was gone. And no one was surprised. All his friends knew he was a control freak. And also because he had given up alcohol two years ago. Suddenly. Just like that.

Before that, he had been cleaning up a botch of scotch, on the rocks, in three days. And he drank every day.

Those were hard times. The family had just moved to Bangalore to see how things would work out there. At night, Yogi and Rupal would put the children to bed. Yogi would then leave for Chennai. Upon reaching the city at 4 a.m., Yogi would catch up on his sleep, waking up again at 8 a.m., to get to office. He would leave Chennai at 4 p.m., getting to Bangalore by 9 p.m., in time to help Rupal put the children to bed. This was his routine three days a week.

And he drank.

Until the day the memory of the three aspiring entrepreneurs working out of the Besant Road apartment years ago in Chennai came rushing back to him, especially of Hari Anna and spasmopoloxin. That was not the path Yogi wanted to go down.

He vowed not to have alcohol until he had achieved something.

He broke that vow when the Series B funding was sealed in February 2015. He would give it up again on 17 March, his birthday.

He does not need alcohol or cigarettes now. The hard days are fast becoming a distant memory. 'I am switched off now. You should have seen me before. Now there are people to do everything. I wanted to build a company that would last. And a company cannot last if there is no structure. Today we have structure, we have people. Six months later, if I get hit by a bus, the company will still grow and achieve its vision.'

And there is Rupal, his wife and colleague, who is with him every step of the way. They got married at twenty-two. It was not an accident. They had talked about it. The clarity with which they approached marriage ensures that a quarrel at home does not come in the way of work, though their differences at work may influence their conversation at home.

'Every person has an office spouse, not necessarily of the opposite gender. They talk to them and rely on them. I think Rupal is as much my wife in the office as at home. She is one of the coolest persons I know.'

Stayzilla's structure is one of shared ownership, but not equal ownership. Whoever is the most capable person can be the CEO, but there can be only one CEO. In its Chennai office, all chairs are identical, only Yogi's is slightly bigger. These props are required to subtly create a consciousness in everyone about who the boss is. That consciousness is important while working with people who are friends, who are close to you, and one of whom is married to you.

'There will always be stuff with close friends and the wife. Some aspect of home might go to office and some aspect of office may come home. But I can proudly say that it was only once that some aspect of home went to office. Most of the time it is the office that comes home. Our arguments at home are about office.'

~

Shashank and Abhinav had met a few investors, all of whom had asked how big the market was. There could not be any answer to that. Practo was the first in the market. Nobody knew the size of the market. 'Look at the traction we are getting,' they would tell investors. 'If this works out, it is going to be so big.'

But investors looked at it technically, like analysts. They were not swayed by the founders' passion, or by their arguments about the enormous talent in India, probably because the young men were just twenty-three, with little work experience.

Shashank used to daydream about meeting an investor who would not ask how big the market was, but would instead ask, 'Why did you do this? What on earth were you thinking, to start this at twenty-two? Why are you fighting so hard?'

Smiling at how unreal his fantasy was, he went to meet Shailendra Singh of Sequoia. As he entered the room and sat down in a chair, Singh asked: 'Why are you doing this? Tell me one thing, you graduated from a good engineering college, why are you setting up a SaaS software in India? Nobody here knows SaaS.'

Shashank took a moment to unbutton his cuffs and roll up his sleeves. For the next hour, he spoke non-stop. He spoke about what he and his mates were doing, why they were doing what they were, why it was important for the world, what they thought they could make from this, and what the next steps were.

Shailendra Singh heard him out quietly. He asked no questions. He did not mention the size of the market. When Shashank stopped speaking, Singh stood up and simply said: 'Okay, we will get you the money. I will ask my team to connect with you and send the paperwork.'

As a mix of relief and exhilaration swept over Shashank, he could only think of Practo's bank account. It was an old account with a four-digit number. Singh was talking about a wire transfer, which needed a modern, technology-enabled account. They would need to open a new bank account fast.

Sequoia had never invested in such a small company. Practo was small, but Singh saw something in it and arranged the seed funding of half-a-million dollars. 'Even today, he believes in what we believe in,' says Shashank.

Singh did not have to regret his decision. Practo used the money to ramp up sales. Its numbers rose ten-fold. In the next round, Series A, another $3.5 million came from Sequoia. This was early 2012. Until then, Practo was a SaaS company. After Series A, it decided it had enough fuel to build a consumer company. It launched practo.com in 2012.

It began very well, but the founders' ambition stretched even further. They invested some capital in Singapore. From the beginning they had wanted to build a global business. 'This is all part of our DNA. It was not like, "Hey, we have money, what do we do with it?" No, we always wanted to be a global company, a consumer company, and we want to have health records.'

The two years from 2012 to 2014 were all about execution. They added ten sales guys and ramped up software sales. The Practo app became one of the most downloaded. It became popular even in Singapore.

In 2014 they met with Matrix. Shashank always thought of Matrix as his preferred investor. He had learned that entrepreneurs understood other entrepreneurs, perhaps also the reason why Shailendra Singh, who had done a couple of start-ups himself, had been open to taking a punt on Practo. Avnish Bajaj, head of Matrix Partners India, knew what it was to be in the shoes of young, inexperienced founders. He had been one. He also had a sharp focus on healthcare.

But it was not love at first meeting. Initially, unlike Singh, Bajaj was not sold on the Practo model. Shashank, too, took his time. He had not known any investor other than Sequoia, which had played a huge role in nurturing Practo over the preceding five years. At every point there was someone from

Sequoia helping them, from doing a television commercial to recruitment.

It was important for both Bajaj and Shashank to know they were working towards the same purpose. They met over dinner and coffee, and spoke with other entrepreneurs. Both liked what they saw and heard and were finally convinced they were made for each other. 'Tomorrow, whether there is a high or a low, these guys are going to do the right thing. Doing the right things is important, it will take you places,' says Shashank.

Bit by bit, meeting by meeting, Bajaj understood what Shashank and Abhinav were trying to do, and got hooked. As a result, Matrix and Sequoia together put in $30 million in 2014. The announcement was made in February 2015, weeks before Shashank and I met at the Oberoi in Bangalore.

Soon Practo would enter the Philippines and Indonesia as part of its international drive. Shashank himself spent time in Singapore, the Philippines and Indonesia to understand the market and the opportunities for Practo.

It helps that Practo sort of started this market, with a strong vision and a passionate team. Attrition is low. The first ten who joined the founders, says Shashank, are still with the company. The first is the head of engineering. The second is sales head, called the head of hunting. The third is the head of India sales. The fourth is a product sales head. The fifth guy is in Singapore.

'What we are building is something bigger than ourselves. I always tell the company that we are building something that is for 100 years, not for the next ten.'

Some people do not see or understand the vision at first, some even poke fun at it, but, given time, it grows on them. Shashank always tells his team that not many will appreciate Practo initially, and might ridicule it, but they will start believing in it once they understand it and use it. He also tells

his people—much in the way Snapdeal's Kunal Bahl does—
that if they tell people what they are doing and people do
not laugh, then they are doing something wrong, or doing
something that is not big enough.

No one laughed when Shashank told his investors he
wanted Practo to be a billion-dollar company. They thought,
'Well, yeah, that might happen.' Later, Shashank said $10
billion. Now they were like, 'Uh oh, what is this?' Still later
he said $100 billion, and they began to laugh: 'Have you lost
your mind?'

'Done,' said Shashank. That, a $100 billion company, is
what he wants to build. What is the point of doing any less?
Anyone can do that.

Yes, it is ambitious, some would even say far-fetched.
Practo's Series B valuation, though extremely impressive for
a start-up, especially a healthcare one, was a far cry, a small
fraction, of a $100 billion dream. But Practo's progress is no
laughing matter.

When Shashank and I met, Practo was growing 20 per cent
month on month. Every four months its numbers were
doubling. It was doing an unbelievable four million searches
a month. That was like Airbnb, the online accommodation
provider, which does more rooms a day than some well-
known global hotel chains. Practo had 120,000 doctors in
thirty-five cities in India.

That makes it several times the size of anyone else in this
business. In fact, it has no real competition. Take Portea, for
instance. Incubated by Krishnan Ganesh and wife, Meena, it
provides doctors, nurses and physiotherapists for home visits.
Practo, on the other hand, is a marketplace where one can
find providers like Portea and choose one of them based on
reviews and recommendations.

Its next target is to be in 100 cities in India, and get into
more countries. As usual, the team is working its ass off.

Kannan, who was an advisor for two years, joined the company as chief operating officer. He has twenty-seven years of experience in running large-scale sales and operations teams. He allows Shashank to focus on product innovation. Abhinav has gone to the United States to set up an innovation lab in San Francisco. He has opened an office there and is hiring, trying to get the best engineers.

'We are solving a global problem,' says Shashank. 'I believe, as I have from the beginning, that this idea is as big as Facebook, LinkedIn, Google. As big and as powerful. That is why we are putting so much into it.'

Abhinav's presence in San Francisco sends out the message that Practo is about innovation. He has taken on the title of chief innovation officer, giving up the earlier one of chief technology officer. 'We are doing multiple things, more than what a company our size can do,' says Shashank.

Few companies have balanced as many things as Practo has: SaaS, a consumer business and an international business. For instance, Zomato, another highly successful start-up, is doing consumer and international businesses, but not SaaS.

'I am a fan of doing an AND, not an OR. For this, my team is always annoyed with me.' That is said with a twinkle in his eye.

Shashank and Abhinav appeared in *Forbes* India's thirty under thirty. That made their parents very proud, but Shashank sees it as a responsibility; they now have to be role models in whatever they do.

At the time we met, Housing.com's Rahul Yadav and his skirmishes with Sequoia were the favourite conversation icebreaker. Shashank, thoughtful as ever, reacts to it, and yet not quite.

'It worries me a lot. It is an ecosystem that has been very competitive. Entrepreneurs are very competitive with each other. We are on this earth for thirty to fifty more years, after which our game is over. Then the next generation takes over. What we are building as the start-up ecosystem is bigger than us. I am not sure all the players understand this.'

Indeed, the start-up system India's entrepreneurs are building can power India. It is what set the United States apart. 'You have to care for both the ecosystem and each person in it. You need to go out of your way to help someone, collaborate. Healthy competition helps all of us. But you can't lose sight of the bigger picture. You have to build a nation that is depending on you in some small way.'

~

In today's day and age, with valuations running into billions, this might sound quaint, but, as recently as a dozen years ago, earning the first million was a big milestone for first-time entrepreneurs. Both Avnish Bajaj and Suvir Sujan came from a middle-class background. When the opportunity to make their first million came their way, as eBay knocked on their door to buy Baazee, it was hard to say no.

Some of their investors were tempted too. It had been a hell of a ride for them. They had come in at the top of the boom and seen things hit rock bottom before getting better. Those four-and-a-half years had felt more like a decade.

Then there was the team, which had stuck it out despite the average pay being 30 per cent to 40 per cent less than the market rate. Baazee either needed to raise money to raise salaries and invest in the business so it could continue with the ride for another four to five years, or answer eBay's call.

The more they thought about it, the more attractive eBay's offer looked. They ended up taking it. The sale was completed in July 2004. The money came within a month.

Actually, a lot of money came. Baazee had raised a total of $21 million from Rupert Murdoch's NewsCorp, steel tycoon Lakshmi Mittal's LNM Internet Ventures, ICICI Ventures, ChrysCapital, and a bunch of lesser known outfits. eBay bought the company for $55 million. A deal of that size for an Internet company was unheard of at the time. It was the largest deal in the consumer technology space in India until Naspers bought redBus in 2012. And it made a lot of people rich.

Everyone in the team had stock options, including the peon, who made Rs 2.2 lakh from the deal. The senior management made ten times their annual salary. 'To be able to come back from the US, bring in the Silicon Valley culture of stock options and see people make money was an end in itself. And, of course, we made more money than we could imagine.'

Avnish stayed on at Baazee as country manager even after it became eBay India. In March 2005, he moved into the role of chairman. He had had a chat with eBay's CEO Meg Whitman about it. The change of role would give him more time and space to do what he had started a few months ago: making small, early investments in start-ups as an angel investor. One of his first investments was in Cleartrip, the online travel services provider. He really enjoyed interacting with entrepreneurs and wanted to do it institutionally.

The Baazee sale had made Avnish a big fish in a small pond. Several venture capitalists were approaching him. A well-known VC from the US came to his office in Mumbai and handed him a signed cheque for $10 million. 'This is for whatever you want to do next,' he said.

This was 2005. The Congress-led United Progressive Alliance had come to power the previous year and, after some hiccups, was off to a good start.

Wondering what to do with his life, Avnish drew up a framework, placing himself at the intersection of skill, opportunity and passion. His belief was that if you had skill and passion but no opportunity, you would be happy but poor. If you had passion and opportunity but not skill, you would be unhappy and unsuccessful. He knew he had to have all three. He also wanted to teach.

That year Avnish visited the US several times on eBay work. On one of those visits, he met a professor of entrepreneurship at Harvard Business School and said he would like to teach there some day. He did not want any money, and he was not the least bit interested in the tenure-track politics that surrounds the appointment of full-time professors. He expected a warm handshake and welcome. What he got was a patronizing pat on the back. 'Join the queue,' the professor said, 'there are 10,000 people ahead of you.'

Avnish did not hold a doctorate in business administration, which was what one needed to teach at Harvard at a young age. Or, one had to be a super achiever. The professor did not think he was one. 'You have made a good start,' the professor said. 'Now you have to excel for the next decade. By that time, hopefully, India will reach a position to have many more courses on it.'

Avnish's wife, Tina, was clear that Avnish had to do a proper job. 'Otherwise, you are just going to sit at home and eat our head.' Teaching was not her idea of a proper job.

Many entrepreneurs would call Avnish for advice, even those not in the Internet space. And they liked what he had to say. His voice anyway carried weight because he had built an organization and had a proven record in operations. He thought he could help people beyond just sharing his knowledge about the Internet.

This passion grew. His skill set became apparent. But Avnish was not clear about the opportunity. So he started his due diligence, meeting scores of people to understand the ecosystem better.

There was one more thing. Though eBay was a fantastic organization, Avnish, while working with it, realized that his temperament was not suited to large organizations. Negotiating for budgets was not his thing. He was more entrepreneurial.

So he picked up the phone and spoke to Whitman. Yes, the understanding with her was that he would stay with eBay India for eighteen months to two years, but could he move on? It was a candid conversation. Whitman said she was fine with it so long as eBay India did not become her problem. Avnish had to ensure a smooth succession.

He did. He became chairman, and slowly began to wind down over the second half of 2005.

Towards the end of the year, he found himself speaking at a Stanford conference in Mumbai. Rishi Navani, who was working with Wentbridge, was also at the conference. They knew each other from the Entrepreneurs Organization meetings. They were both part of the EO sub-group called Forum. They chatted a lot at the Stanford conference.

Before the year was out, Rishi got in touch with Avnish to say he was leaving Wentbridge. 'How about doing something together?'

They talked some more. Two months later they became partners. They were to start their own firm in January 2006. But as the US woke up from its holiday slumber, the VCs who had been talking to Avnish were back on the phone with him again. One of them was Matrix.

'I have moved on,' Avnish told Matrix. 'I have partnered with someone else to set up a fund.'

'Why don't you both partner with us?' asked Matrix. So Avnish went to the US with Rishi to talk to Matrix.

It was love at first sight, which survived the test of a few more meetings. They agreed to join hands, despite all the advice Avnish had received about joint ventures across geographies being doomed to failure.

'The decision was made on trust,' he says. 'It has really worked well.'

Matrix Partners India was launched in July 2006. It announced its first fund in August. Avnish left eBay India in early 2007. Today Matrix India has two funds with $600 million under management. It has made fifty investments in the last nine years, exited a few, and has close to forty active portfolios.

Early on it played safe, and made more mid-market investments. In the last few years, it has become more of a VC. Avnish was still making personal investments when Matrix was doing mainly mid-market deals, but not anymore. He has not made a personal investment since 2007–08.

'I would say—and this is not to be immodest—we are the number one VC in the country, not only in strike rate but also in value creation,' says Avnish.

The facts are in his favour. You would have heard about his investments in the news: Quikr, Ola, LimeRoad, Practo, Stayzilla, Dailyhunt and more. These are the stars of Indian Internet start-ups, already valued high and growing. In all of them, Matrix invested very early. Quikr was pretty much conceived in the Matrix office.

'One feather in the cap I am happy to be immodest about is that I have never lost money on the Internet. Probably, after this statement made to you, I will lose money,' says Avnish, as both of us laugh and clutch our wooden tables so as not to tempt fate.

He was very close to losing money in one of his investments, Exclusively.in, but Myntra bought it. So Avnish got Myntra shares and ended up making money. (After Flipkart bought Myntra, the founders of Exclusively.in bought the company back; they later sold it to Snapdeal.)

The secret to Avnish's 100 per cent strike rate is actually no secret at all. 'The art of good investing lies in applying a framework, which is common sense, but applying it consistently and persistently, as opposed to developing a new framework.'

Here are the nuances. Every investor says that what he looks for in an investee company is the right team, market, business model, sustainable differentiation, deal and pricing. But some investors are putting their money in the market more than in a team, which they are ready to build. Another lot invests in the team, irrespective of the market. Avnish is more biased towards the team, but he has to believe in the market. 'If a team I love is chasing a market I do not believe in, I will see if I can convince them to take a small amount of money and wait until my thesis or theirs on the market is proved right. If they want a large cheque, I will walk away even if the team is great. But if there is a great market and an average team, I will never invest. I start with the team but I have to believe that the team's and my views of the market converge at some point.'

Ola is a great example. Avnish really liked Bhavish Aggarwal, its founder. He was clear that he was going to work with Bhavish. But every time he looked at the market and business model, he had doubts. There were questions about how the business would make money, there was regulatory overhang, fuel prices were high, and taxi drivers were not making money.

Finally, he told Bhavish: 'I want to work with you. If you want to work with me, we must have the same view on all the issues that need to be dealt with and fixed, so that at the end of this we are not at loggerheads.'

'Absolutely,' said Bhavish. 'I want to do the right thing and I believe the same thing.'

They came together.

∼

By the end of 2014, Paytm needed more money. It had raised a total of just $18 million till then from Intel Capital, SAIF and some others. By now the other companies were spending pots of money to get more and more users through marketing and discounts. So Vijay Shekhar Sharma went on a roadshow to meet influential investors in New York, San Francisco, Singapore, and Hong Kong.

He met Jack Ma, founder of the Chinese Internet behemoth Alibaba group, in late October 2014 in Hangzhou. The meeting was arranged by a founding member of SAIF partners. Vijay had heard Ma once, in 2011, as part of the audience at a *Wall Street Journal* event in Hong Kong, where Ma had talked about his business growing from $64 billion to $126 billion in just a year.

Vijay was at once incredulous and star-struck. He decided to read everything he could find on Jack Ma and Alibaba, AliExpress, Alipay and Taobao. By the time he got the chance to meet Ma in Hangzhou, he was prepared. Scheduled to last twenty minutes, their meeting went on for two hours, by the end of which Ma had decided to invest in Paytm.

What did Ma really like about Vijay and his company?

'The hardship I had gone through. He actually said during that meeting that when he should want to enter India, he would take a fledgling entrepreneur for a partner rather than a large company. He believed that entrepreneurs who had gone through hardship built great companies.'

Ma was true to his word. In February 2015, Ant Financial, an Alibaba affiliate, invested $575 million in One97. Seven months later, in September, Alibaba invested directly, along with Ant Financial, a reported $680 million more. But Vijay, by virtue of being the only founder and not having raised too much money early on, still has 21 per cent equity.

These investments create an intriguing situation. Alibaba is also an investor in Snapdeal. What's more, Japan's

SoftBank, Snapdeal's largest investor, owns nearly 35 per cent of Alibaba. Snapdeal has moved into the mobile payments business by acquiring FreeCharge, coming toe to toe with Paytm.

In fact, Vijay sounds just like Kunal when talking about making life easier for small merchants. Kunal speaks about a merchant in Surat, Vijay talks about one in Vadodara. 'This guy sitting in Vadodara has a price benefit. In his store he can match the lowest prices. But he does not know how to ship his wares to various nooks and corners of the country, and he does not know how to collect payments.'

Here, Vijay adds a twist. Cash on delivery, which has been the one great innovation in Indian commerce and dominates transactions at many large outfits, is not reliable. 'Can a small merchant leave a Rs 40,000 phone in thin air and wait several days for the money to come to him?'

A rhetorical question, as the fellow obviously cannot. Vijay's wallets and payment platform solve this problem. This shows up in the high prepaid component in Paytm's transactions. 'At other companies, 70 per cent of the business consists of cash-on-delivery orders. On Paytm, 90 per cent is prepaid.'

Kunal Bahl will be trying to catch up on this front. FreeCharge, after Snapdeal acquired it, has started a mobile wallet. It claimed to have sold a million of these wallets within five days of launch.

One business distinction for Vijay can be the dominance of mobile in Paytm's transactions—quite fitting for a company which, it will be fair to say, found its calling in the mobile phone from the very beginning. 'Nearly all of our business is done on the mobile. There is very little on the web, though we do have a website. We started with the mobile.'

Heck, he once had a T-shirt that said: 'Born mobile, going places'.

Last heard, he was trying to take Paytm outside India. Paytm is said to be working with AliExpress, Alibaba's international online marketplace, to tap international markets. This could make Paytm India's first online marketplace to go international.

Between the two Alibaba investments came Ratan Tata's. Vijay had been advised to meet Tata, who can be a fantastic brand ambassador for whichever company he invests in. A meeting was arranged, which, like the one with Ma, went on for much longer than planned. At the end of it, Tata agreed to not only invest but also to become an advisor.

Incidentally, one of Tata's first investments in e-commerce was in Snapdeal.

~

CHAPTER 7

Sandeep Aggarwal, Radhika's husband and the force behind ShopClues, was arrested by agents of the United States Federal Bureau of Investigation in San Jose, California, on 30 July 2013. He was charged with insider trading by the Southern District of New York administration. The US Securities & Exchange Commission, too, accused him of divulging details about the progress of the Microsoft–Yahoo negotiations in July 2009. Later, according to the charges, he tipped SAC Capital Advisors' portfolio manager, Richard Lee, about a pending deal between Microsoft and Yahoo.

Lee pleaded guilty to the insider trading charges for receiving non-public information in July 2009 that contained confidential talks between Yahoo and Microsoft. He became the fifth former SAC employee to cooperate with the United States government's investigation into the hedge fund firm accused of insider trading.

The SEC said Aggarwal had learned confidential and vital details about the progress of the Microsoft–Yahoo negotiations in 2009 from a close friend in Microsoft.

Sanjay Wadhwa, senior associate director of the SEC's New York Regional Office, said in a press release that as a sell-side analyst, Aggarwal knew the rules and yet broke them. Preet Bharara, the US attorney for the Southern District of New York, said in a statement: 'We continue our work to investigate and prosecute privileged professionals who think the laws requiring honesty and fair play do not apply to them.'

Radhika cannot talk about the case since it is still sub judice. She would only say: 'Sandeep is working with the government. He is cooperating with the Southern District of New York. It was the most benign case.'

Still, it changed many things at ShopClues. After all, Sandeep was critical to it. He was the 'vision' guy. The others, however, were working at a frenetic pace. The team stuck together. They were all data-oriented and kept records of everything. It is easier to execute when you can measure the results of what you are doing, note where things are going well and where they might be falling off. Sandeep provided guidance from the outside from time to time.

Sanjay and Radhika stepped up and took on larger roles. Sanjay, who was the COO, became CEO in Sandeep's place. Radhika, who had been only doing the marketing, took on a lot of the strategic aspects. It wasn't easy.

'We were growing very fast till then. It took me two to three months to even get back on track. I could not figure out what to do. Sandeep was stuck in the US. Everything went awry. Nobody had any idea it was coming. You plan for accidents, medical emergencies—this is not something you plan for. I don't know anyone to whom such a thing has happened. It does not even seem real. It is as though I am looking at someone else's life.'

At first it was about survival. Radhika took a month and a half to deliberate whether to move back to the US—and therefore out of ShopClues—where Sandeep was holed up. In the end she decided not to, and is glad for it.

'Till date we are doing very well. We are just blessed.'

It did delay funding though—and everything else, for e-commerce depends a lot on the money coming in. It was early 2014 by the time ShopClues raised another round, Series C, of $20 million. Nexus, Helion and one new investor, whose identity would not be disclosed, brought in the money.

This is where the ShopClues founders, with their team spirit and doggedness, shine. Quite in contrast were the founders of Yebhi.com, an early, bright star of e-commerce in India, who bickered to the bitter end. Radhika talks to many budding entrepreneurs who come to her for advice. She tells them capital is important, but the most important factor is the team.

Of course, the ShopClues founders were more mature than many start-up founders of the day who were in their mid- to late twenties. They were mature enough to consider the prospect of failure. They thought they would go back and take up jobs if things did not seem to be working out after six months.

They were also thick. So much so that Mrinal moved on at the end of 2014 for personal reasons. But he remains close friends with the rest.

These guys also had experience and pedigree, having worked in blue chip companies. They had skills as well as a social and corporate community to back them up.

That is how Nexus came in. Narendra Gupta, one of its top guys, who sits in California, knew Sandeep professionally. He knew about his plans for ShopClues and was always interested. Nexus moved in quickly at the early signs of traction.

The traction played a role in interesting ways. Radhika and Sandeep were in Hong Kong, meeting investors. One of the investors confessed to them that he did not, at first, wish to meet them at all. But a visit to his home town in Amritsar changed his mind. His eleven-year-old niece was looking for basketball shoes. 'Where can we find basketball shoes for an eleven-year-old?' this investor asked around people.

'Try ShopClues,' said the niece.

'I have heard of these guys,' thought the investor, who had been approached by investment bankers for the meeting just a little earlier. 'I should meet them.' He was not the only one to show interest in the venture. Helion and Nexus brought in more money in early 2015, and Tiger Global also got on board. They brought in a combined $100 million.

'Whatever has happened, the investors have stood by us.'

But what about the first investor, the one that had ditched them that Tuesday evening in August 2011?

'They had last-minute jitters, I think,' says Radhika, and chuckles. 'They have not been able to invest in India up till today. Let me assure you, it was a bad move by them.'

What about the rumours that ShopClues could be bought over by Flipkart, since Tiger is common to both?

'No, no, no,' she says, terrified at the thought. 'You can't merge us with Flipkart. Try and imagine putting Karol Bagh and DLF Emporio together. It is not going to work.'

Sixty-five per cent of ShopClues' sales come from tier-2 and tier-3 towns. It is all about Etawah, Coimbatore, Ranchi. Growing up, Radhika lived in some of those places. Sanjay's father, too, had a transferable job and he had lived and studied in places like Jhansi and Allahabad.

The couple know their small towns. Radhika visited Pune, where she was born, and loved it so much she ended up buying an apartment there.

'We will remain Karol Bagh online. The goal is to remain mass market, regional brand-oriented. That is our bread and butter. That market is untapped. Nobody is even looking at it. Our competitors say they are in tier-2 and tier-3, but none of them is truly there.'

ShopClues penetrates these markets with its large number of merchants who establish these regional and local brands. As a random example, if you are looking to buy a lunch box, ShopClues would have one from Tupperware priced at, say, Rs 550. There will also be a Topware, to be had for a little less. The typical ShopClues customer is more likely to buy Topware despite the not-so-large price difference.

'They want a brand, but are highly value conscious.' So Topware will do.

Apparel is a big category for ShopClues, but it would leave the finery to Myntra, Jabong or LimeRoad. Home furnishing is another big one. A hot-selling bedsheet on ShopClues would be priced at, say, Rs 350, instead of, say, Rs 800 or Rs 1500, which it tends to be on other sites.

'If you look at the largest selection of shoes under Rs 500, we have pretty decent ones. I have used them.'

No way, I say, she is likely to wear Prada.

'I do like my Prada, but I do buy from ShopClues.'

Fairly regularly, actually. She places orders frequently and also talks to customer support. What better way to check the processes? 'I am not my target customer. But I do understand my customer.'

So how was her customer experience at ShopClues? 'Not always good,' she concedes. 'We do mess up.'

Sandeep, meanwhile, is spending more and more time in India, investing in start-ups. He retains his holding in ShopClues, which is separate from Radhika's, but has not resumed an active role.

He set up Droom, an online marketplace for automobiles, in 2014. He has also invested in Shopsity, which provides information on fashion products being sold in stores in the user's vicinity through a mobile app. Shopsity's founder, Danish Ahmed, was the one who had started Yebhi.com, before Manmohan and Nitin took charge of it.

~

'Are you mad?' the chartered accountant asked Suchi Mukherjee. 'You are new, you are a woman, you have been working abroad, you don't know this country. Please go back.'

This CA had come recommended by Suchi's friends in England. So it was a rude shock to hear him speak like that. 'I was so flabbergasted. It is difficult to put someone like me in a position where I stop speaking. You have to bludgeon me on my head. That CA made me speechless.'

Of course, she was in no mood to take his advice and go back. So she just found another CA. Then she ended meeting with some engineers.

She had come to India thinking that she could knock on any door and engineers would tumble out from it. They still might have, but not the kind she was hoping for. 'Indians are genetically sharp. But our education system kills us. It is a system trained to kill our brain cells.'

Finally, one day, she told two of her recruiters that she was not leaving a corner coffee shop in Koramangala, Bangalore, until she had found some good engineers. They started with back-to-back interviews in the morning and finished late in the evening.

At the end of the day, a man who had spent the entire day at the next table with his computer told Suchi: 'That was one hell of a speed dating session.'

Suchi had set the bar high. Finally, when she had assembled a five-member engineering team, they were all under twenty-seven and had studied computer science at IIT. Three of them held patents and had run their own businesses.

Finding co-founders had been a tad easier. Friends introduced her to Manish Saxena, who knew retail and had been with Tommy Hilfiger; Ankush Mehra, a hardcore supply chain guy who had worked with Reliance, and Prashant Malik, who took his time but eventually moved from the valley in early 2013.

LimeRoad was launched in late 2012. Suchi had moved her family to Delhi in April that year. Barclays, where Sandeep had joined in 2009, sent him there in December.

The surest prod for the move came in June 2011, when Bejul Somaia of Lightspeed Venture Partners met Suchi in London and said: 'Here is some money, just do this.'

He was one of the initial investors Suchi had met. She had kept bouncing ideas off Somaia, but it was not easy to take the leap. Life was good in England. Things had a settled look about them, down to the Indian help at home.

The first thing Suchi did after Somaia offered her money was to call up Ahti Heinla, the chief founding architect of Skype, with whom she had worked. 'You have made a lot of money. Why don't we build something disruptive out of India?' Heinla considered the idea for a long time, and became a small investor in LimeRoad, but he would not move to India.

Suchi began to travel to India, spending two weeks a month there. She resigned from eBay in September 2011, after her maternity leave ended. For the next year or so, she did all kinds of research. She found that India accounted for 21 per cent of global manufacturing in lifestyle products at factory prices. 'That is huge! India doesn't account for 21 per cent of anything in the world, not even population.'

What if this 21 per cent of lifestyle could be online, in a way that was magically browsable? It could create the largest discovery platform out of India.

Discovery is hard. It is easy to discover a Blackberry or an iPhone. But no woman says, 'Today I have to buy the cheapest black dress.' She would say a lot more: about the neckline, frills, sleeves, no sleeves, halter neck, plunging neck, maxi, mini, shorts, lace, no lace, cotton, silk, raw silk . . .

Suchi figured that users would help with discovery. So she went out to find her users, often with Heinla, an Estonian, by her side. With the help of Third Eye, a research company, they visited several homes, trying to understand what women in India bought, how they made purchases and how often. They went to all kinds of localities of different income groups: Delhi's Rajouri Garden, Faridabad, Gurgaon, Bandra in Mumbai and so on. Suchi spoke on the phone with women in Allahabad and other non-metro cities.

She realized that the women she had met in Rajouri Garden were distinctly different from the women she spoke to in, say, Greater Kailash, even though they were in the same age group and were living in the same city. They thought differently, spoke differently, behaved differently and, importantly for Suchi, shopped and dressed differently.

Suchi went into the warehouses of the large logistics companies to see how they managed and moved stock, and recorded traffic speeds to assess movement of goods. Then she started doing research on talent. Did people really want to join start-ups? It was a legitimate question at the time. Thankfully, the answer was yes. Avnish Bajaj, who would invest in LimeRoad, had become a known name for his success with Baazee and his successful exit from it; Deep Kalra had done an IPO for MakeMyTrip. They had become role models.

But neither example would console Anjali, Suchi's mother. When Suchi joined Lehman, a global investment bank, her mother thought she was set-up for life, for a long ride on the gravy train. When Suchi decided to leave Lehman and join eBay, her mother thought she was giving up her career. She liked Skype, though, because she used it. Gumtree, she thought, was a waste of Suchi's time. But nothing had prepared her for LimeRoad.

It was a new low for Anjali when Suchi told her she was going to set up her own company. That was something only children of business families did, or politicians did, or other people who had some way of obtaining a licence.

That made Suchi conscious of how parents react to their children joining start-ups. So LimeRoad has an insurance policy that covers elderly parents of employees. It reassures parents who ask their children what on earth they are joining. The children can always say: 'It's not an MNC, it's not a bank, it's not government, Ma, but they give insurance for you.'

There is an employee in the company's supply chain whose parents call one of the co-founders at least once a quarter to ask how the company is doing. And the co-founders tell them not to worry, that the company is well-funded.

That is true of LimeRoad, thanks to Suchi's track record and that of the other co-founders. It needed no seed capital or angel funding. It raised $5 million straightaway in Series A, and then $15 million in Series B.

'We got cash on the basis of who we were and what we had done. In Series B, we got more than what we wanted, though the markets were pretty bad.'

At the time I met Suchi, LimeRoad was growing at a furious pace. So was its community. The scrapbookers were happily doing their own thing. The vendors were coming in on their own; LimeRoad did not guarantee them any sales.

Recently, the head of a company called Suchi to say he wanted to build a community just like LimeRoad's. What kind of skills should he look for in his community manager? That was a difficult question. One of Suchi's community managers was a girl straight out of the National Institute of Fashion Design. She had experience only in photography. She just happened to have the nous for managing communities.

Community building was happening elsewhere too, notably around Suchi's daughter at her school, Sanskriti, in New Delhi's Chanakyapuri. School did not get off to a good start for Suchi's daughter. She returned from her first day at the school with a look of horror on her face.

'How was your day?' Suchi asked.

'It's so noisy.'

That's the last thing Suchi could have thought would be her daughter's complaint. 'Yet, at that point I knew I had done the right thing in coming back.' Her child was no longer growing up in a cultural bubble.

~

'We have a slightly unique approach to e-commerce,' says Kunal Bahl. 'Traditionally, e-commerce in India and most parts of the world has been monolithic. You can do everything on one platform: watch movies, buy stuff, buy services. That era is ending, especially given the mobile.'

We are in a small conference room at 238, Phase III, Okhla, New Delhi. This is April 2015. We are sitting in a really tiny conference room with a centre table whose top is really thin. Some chairs, equally fragile, have been placed around it. Kunal is wearing what looks like newly acquired spectacles. They add an element of seriousness to the thirty-two-year-old's boyish face, but only until he begins to laugh. He still has a boy's laughter.

But what is the way ahead as e-commerce comes of age?

It is Facebook's way. The social media giant talks of its business as a clan of apps. Facebook is a monolith—you can do everything on it, from photo sharing and messaging to searching. Yet, it has built a family of apps, such as WhatsApp and Instagram, through acquisition. In a world that is going mostly mobile, all these app icons on a user's mobile represent something. They have an association with the user, which plays out in their choice of clicking them. That choice goes in an app's favour as it is specific and provides the best-in-class experience.

'Social networks are a strong, leading indicator of how e-commerce will evolve. Not a monolithic platform, but an ecosystem or a set of apps.'

Kunal, in fact, does not see Snapdeal as an e-commerce company. He sees it as one that enables others to do e-commerce. There are a few things every small business in India needs, but cannot possibly organize on its own. These requirements include a merchandising platform, logistics support, traffic, customer support, payment support and mobile commerce compatibility. Snapdeal wants to provide them with a platform that has all these features.

Already, some small businesses on Snapdeal are making twice the turnover they used to earlier. These are small guys selling sarees, or some Nehru Place chap selling gadgets. 'When I was in college, they used to teach us mission, values and vision. I thought it was mumbo jumbo. It's only in the last one year that I have started realizing the value of that teaching. The soul of our business is in creating life-changing experiences for these small businesses.'

For consumers, the value proposition is certain availability of products at the lowest prices.

In doing what it has, Snapdeal has overturned the e-commerce concept. The business has three pillars: value, convenience and assortment (or selection). Most e-commerce companies have focused on convenience as their number one concern by a long yard, followed by value as a distant second. Selection is often only the third concern.

Snapdeal decided it could not be everything to everyone, but could certainly be many things to many people. It identified assortment and selection as the biggest issues arising from the low penetration of retail in India. It put assortment as number one, followed by value and convenience.

'Not that we were inconvenient. We will deliver within the time frame in which we tell you we will deliver. But we won't do edgy things like delivering in six hours. We would rather be the absolute leaders in assortment and value.'

When a consumer searches for something on Snapdeal and does not find it, a report goes to the Snapdeal team, which tries to bring in that product at the earliest. 'It is a daily thing. If you want an air fryer, we have it. It is a weird product, not very popular. But if you search for a product and find it on the site, you are likely to search for other products on the same site. Availability becomes a hook. The focus on certainty of availability has really paid off.'

This could not have been done in an inventory-led model, which requires the e-commerce outfit to have stocks of goods sold on its platform.

Secondly, most e-commerce companies focus on the urban elite. Their hypothesis is not wrong. They are the people with money, credit cards, computers, Internet connectivity and aspiration. Yet, they are people who, if they need to buy something, can go out in a car (driven by someone else), to a swanky mall and do experiential shopping. They have no dearth of access to goods.

Middle India has an access problem. It has rising income, but no access to objects of its desire. Naturally, they would be most eager to take to online shopping. Snapdeal reached out to them.

That entailed control over the shipping. A lot of e-commerce companies start their own logistics companies. Snapdeal did not want to. It adds to the overheads and recurring operational expenditure without improving anyone's life, certainly not of the delivery boy, who would make the same money whether it is paid by a logistics company or an e-commerce company.

Instead, Snapdeal wanted to control the intelligent portion of the supply chain. So, it created a reverse auction marketplace called Safe Ship for courier companies. All of them, small and large, would be on one side and all the sellers on the other.

Once an order is placed, it goes to a seller's panel. The seller presses a button to generate a packing slip, which has a courier company and a barcode already assigned through a dynamic system based on the historical service quality and cost for the address where the delivery has to be made.

If three courier companies are servicing a lane, the system picks the one which has provided the best service in that lane at the lowest cost. The seller then packs the item in a Snapdeal-branded box and sticks a label on it. The courier company picks it up and scans it. Once scanned, the customer, seller and Snapdeal can track it.

'Without anyone taking on the burden of owning a logistics company and without our owning the product, we are able to provide the same experience that any inventory-led business could possibly provide.'

The money the consumer pays, whether electronic or cash, first comes to Snapdeal before it goes to the seller. It sits in an escrow, which Snapdeal calls Trust Pay Guarantee, for seven days during which it can get refunded to the customer if he has a problem with the product. This is inspired by Alibaba's system Alipay.

'Our business is so much about trust driven by policy. Trust does not get built by saying "trust me", or by calling something trustworthy. It is built by the right policies.'

Snapdeal has to earn not just one customer's trust, but that of two for each transaction. The seller, too, is Snapdeal's customer and, in fact, the one that pays money to be on its platform. Snapdeal makes money from the seller and not the buyer of products.

It did consider, in the beginning, whether to charge sellers for listing their products, but decided against it. It wanted to make money only when the ecosystem made money. 'We are an ecosystem player and we have to make sure we are balanced with everyone, even with courier companies.'

Snapdeal's ecosystem has grown dramatically, aided by acquisition.

~

CHAPTER 8

'Our offerings to the consumer are under three heads: pay, buy, and save. Under "save", we are going to act as the facilitator for a range of financial services. We have applied for a payments bank licence . . . '

Vijay Shekhar Sharma, talking animatedly to me on 20 August 2015, was in the middle of that sentence on Thursday when his mobile phone rang. The caller told him the Reserve Bank of India (RBI) had granted him the licence he had just mentioned.

Squealing with joy and making thumbs-up gestures, Sharma rushed out of the room to celebrate with his team and to take calls from television channels. It was a while before he could return to resume our interview.

It was a big day in the life of the young company, the youngest in the list of eleven who got the RBI's licence to start a payments banks, which can do some of what a full-fledged bank does, such as deposits and payments, but cannot give loans. Paytm was also the only e-commerce outfit on that list.

But ten others had obtained this licence. And there is also a large number of universal banks. How will Paytm's bank be distinctive?

'We know there will be a need for many elements like banking correspondents and bank branches, but we will be primarily led by the mobile,' said Sharma. 'The consumer will get a very different experience of mobile banking.'

Paytm already had 100 million mobile wallets, more than anyone else by a long mile. How could the wallet users be an asset to its other businesses? 'That is the "pay" part. We can graduate those consumers to "buy", when they can transact on our online market platform. The same set of customers can move to financial services, or the "save" part of our platform. By using technology, we can contribute to financial inclusion.'

That adds a nice touch to the career of a man who once found raising loans the biggest stumbling block in the path to his dreams. He still considers it the single biggest problem for aspiring entrepreneurs. 'In India, it is easy to get a Rs 1000 crore loan, but not so easy to get a Rs 6 lakh loan.'

What do his parents think of his work now? 'They don't feel bad, they don't feel bad,' Vijay says, amid peals of laughter. Then he composes himself. 'We have built something worthwhile. Once in a lifetime, God gives you the opportunity to make a dent in the universe. That's how I look at it.'

And what does he think of his Hindi-to-English-medium transition?

'Oh, education is overrated. I studied in the Hindi medium. Then I went to an engineering college. Education there did not happen in the classroom. The classroom was not a very comforting environment for me. Curriculum education is overrated. The real education is learning from experience and case studies. The system of cramming some words and terms and achieving a rank based on that is overrated. Rank does not reflect the capability of a person. You would know what the book says, but you wouldn't know how to live life, my friend.'

~

In a nutshell, Avnish is entrepreneur-driven, but to invest in someone, he or she has to be an intellectually honest entrepreneur. 'I have to feel that if things don't align over a period of time, they will listen to me. If that is the case, they will likely get me excited enough to invest, even if it is the shittiest market out there.'

What is it that he likes in an entrepreneur? 'I like them young and fearless, because a lot of what we are doing today is innovation. It has not been done before. Sometimes, guys who have been working for a while have too much baggage, too much unlearning to do.'

It is not that he abhors the experienced ones. But he likes them coming out of great training grounds like Google, Amazon and eBay. And he likes both types, the young and the experienced, to be product-oriented.

'The best products win. So I look for product-obsessed founders—missionary and visionary, not mercenary.' Missionaries and visionaries attract the best of talent, which tends to stick together during the worst of times because they can rally around the founder. They also build to last, not to exit. And if the founder is also smart, hardworking, intellectually honest and has high integrity, everything falls in place.'

Among markets, he likes the ones where the product fit is obvious. Ola, again, is the perfect example. All of us have faced pain in the world of cabs. It was a system waiting to be fixed—disrupted, rather, in the start-up language. It was an unlimited demand kind of market at which you just had to point the right product.

If the formula is that simple, can anyone become a successful VC? Apparently not. Avnish's formula appears simple and replicable, but its application and success is down to the individual. For instance, what Avnish looks for in an entrepreneur is pretty much what he finds in himself. 'This business cannot be taught, but it can be learned. I was a terrible investor at first. What I am telling you is what I have learned. And the implementation of the framework has to come internally. At the precise moment, you have to say yes or no to an investment. That moment, that judgement, that critical thinking, is what defines our business. My own critical thinking has evolved significantly. And I am still learning.'

Mistakes have contributed immensely to that learning. At the end of 2009, he invested in a microfinance company in Andhra Pradesh. Avnish really liked the founder. But the venture failed. Candid as ever, Avnish says that the reason for the failure was Andhra Pradesh's decision to change the rules of microfinance, which killed several companies in that space in the state. But that was not the whole truth.

'The truth is that I invested too late in that sector. It had become very hot. The philosophy there was FOMO (fear of missing out) or JOMO (jealousy on missing out). I felt we had missed out. I let external pressure and internal pressure to do something in that sector override my better judgement. My judgement is that it was overheated.'

He had seen a report that said the average household in Andhra Pradesh had taken loans from four to five micro-finance companies and was using one to repay the other. But this had been going on for five or six years now and appeared to be par for the course. The reality is that in the absence of that evergreening, the business would have survived even after the state had changed the rules of the game. 'But I overlooked it because our business is a classic, fear-versus-greed business. In this case, I was greedy and I did not know when to recognize fear and greed in others and in myself.'

Neither fear nor greed drove Avnish's investments in e-commerce during the lull of 2011–13, when very few were willing to bet on the sector. As the Sensex fell and the real estate sector went into a slumber, e-commerce funding dried up and start-ups began to stutter. But Avnish recognized it as nothing but a fear cycle. Matrix invested the most in the sector in 2012–13.

His mistakes have also taught him to stay clear of two types of entrepreneurs. One is the entrepreneur of less-than-excellent capabilities. Earlier, Avnish would invest in a venture headed by an entrepreneur of average proficiency if the market looked strong. Avnish would think he could teach the entrepreneur. That is the classic mistake of an operational person turned investor.

The second type of entrepreneur is the type he instinctively distrusts. Avnish has often come across situations where the entrepreneur was talented and the market strong, but for some reason that he could not pinpoint, he could not bring himself to trust the fellow. Each time he invested in such a company, it turned out to be a bad decision.

Avnish does not entertain either type of entrepreneur anymore. There are companies he has passed up that have become successful, but he has no regrets. 'I have always been a big believer in the journey being the destination, and there are certain people with whom I do not want to make the journey. I know the journey will be painful for both sides, and I don't want it, irrespective of how talented the guy is, how big the market is, what my people are saying, or what people outside are saying—I just won't do it.'

So what does the wiser Avnish see when he looks back?

For all his professional adventures, it is a personal milestone that he considers the highlight of his life: his children.

'Tomorrow, if I get recognized as the best VC in the country, frankly, it won't be because of me, but because of the entrepreneurs. Both my destiny as well as my balls are in their hands.'

His lowest point in life, too, is personal: the death of his father. The stupid arrest does not even come close.

~

At the beginning of every financial quarter, Snapdeal's senior team defines its mission. The method for setting this mission can hardly be described as scientific. In fact, the acronym for the approach is BHAG, which stands for 'big, hairy, audacious goal'. Once the targets are set, Kunal goes out into the main hall of the office lined with rows and rows of desks and announces them.

'Unless they start to sweat with anxiety or laugh out loud at its ridiculousness, the mission is not high enough. If it takes someone just five minutes to think of a way to achieve it, we haven't aimed high enough,' he says.

The announcement is followed by a ten-day planning process during which every team decides how it will achieve its mission. The teams then hole themselves up in a room for two days, Friday and Saturday, and make presentations on how they will achieve their mission. That creates accountability and galvanizes everyone.

Most of the team members only know about the company's current quarterly mission, which they concentratedly work on. In a business that is changing rapidly, it is only the core team that concerns itself with annual plans. 'In our business, six months is like three years.'

It certainly felt that way in 2013. Snapdeal had a Mission 24 for the July–September period that year. Its target was to start shipping out 75 per cent of all orders within twenty-four hours of their placement. In June that year, just before Mission 24 began, a mere 22 per cent of the orders were shipping out within twenty-four hours. Raising this to 75 per cent across thousands of products and thousands of towns and cities was a crazy target. All the company's sellers and couriers had to change the way they worked. Alert systems to flag breaches had to be set in place.

Yet the team went hard at it, achieving an astounding 80 per cent by September.

Snapdeal is very mindful of what it must not do. For instance, it will not do logistics, although that is one of the three pillars of e-commerce. The logic is simple: doing logistics would take manpower and resources away from its core business. Instead, it should leave logistics to the logistics companies. If e-commerce companies shipped millions of products every month, courier and logistics companies were bound to take notice and make sure they did not lose out on the opportunity.

They did—to the extent that many of them have their chief financial officers visiting e-commerce offices every month for joint business planning, route planning, network expansion, redundancy planning, etc. The e-commerce companies declare things like untapped potential, that if they were to start serving a certain PIN code in Gujarat, there could be 200 deliveries to be made from the very next day to that area. These things come in handy for courier companies, at a time when document deliveries are declining because of the increasing usage of digital documents and transfers.

In fashion, Snapdeal did not focus too much on the upmarket brands. Instead, it focused on the right products for the right target audience. It went for the long-tail of fashion brands, which account for 97 per cent of fashion sales in India, which, in reality, are not really established brands. Typically, these are saree guys in Surat or Varanasi, T-shirt guys in Tirupur, shoe guys in Agra.

Think how their lives must have changed. The saree guy in Surat makes a piece for Rs 350 and sells it in his city for Rs 500–550. The same saree will probably sell for Rs 1700 in the wholesale market of Delhi's Chandni Chowk. On Snapdeal it might sell for Rs 800 with free shipping to anywhere in the country.

All the four parties in this transaction benefit: the guy who made the saree, the one who delivered it, the one who marketed it and the one who bought it. Everyone else is ancillary to the transaction. 'In our country, middlemen are sucking the life out of the economy. We are helping in intermediation. You need someone to connect the dots,' says Kunal. He meets a seller a week to keep his finger on the pulse of the trade.

A vast majority of Snapdeal's sellers use the mobile app made for them. Snapdeal tells them the best price of a product. If they can match it, all they need to do is to press a button. This is done through analytics.

'That is the true value of a marketplace. It drives down prices naturally through healthy competition. That's the big reason we will never compete against our sellers.'

Kunal is careful not to do anything that will scare away his sellers or buyers. Mobile phone usage burgeoned when, among other developments, local languages began to be supported on their platforms. Even someone who understands English may prefer to browse in their mother tongue. Snapdeal has embraced many languages other than English. When we met in April 2015, 7 per cent of its traffic was in Hindi and Tamil. Four more languages were about to be introduced.

And then there are the acquisitions.

~

Phanindra and family were denied UK visas the first time they applied for them. There was not enough money in their HDFC bank account. How were they going to fund the trip? And what would they want to come back to?

Their wealth advisor told them to apply again, this time with the details of their Citibank account, which was host to the money from Ibibo. The visas were granted now, and the family booked their tickets.

Phani's mobile phone did not have international roaming. He bought a Matrix card, but got stuck in the authentication process. It would have taken just a little more effort to activate his mobile service, but that seemed unnecessary.

The vipassana had taught him years ago to detach himself. When he went to attend conferences in China or Singapore, he would check email only occasionally. Even when he visited Nizamabad on short breaks, he would more or less switch off.

There was nothing to worry about in London anyway. A good two months had passed since the deal with Ibibo was announced. Alok Goel had been granted his dear wish and made the chief operating officer.

By the time Phani came back to Bangalore, two senior managers, Goel and Satish Gidugu, the chief technology officer, wanted to quit. Phani was not surprised at Gidugu's decision. He had already told Phani he missed the start-up culture of the old redBus and wanted to move on. But why Goel?

Phani had gone out of his way to push Goel's case for the post of COO. True, Goel was not becoming a millionaire overnight, but that was never on the cards. He had not yet completed a year in redBus, and the shares of his ESOPs had not yet come to him. Still, Ibibo had given him a fat salary hike and a retention bonus that would easily take care of the ESOP loss. Only, the bonus, like all retention bonuses, would come at the end of the financial year.

It was clear that the big reason Ibibo bought redBus was its team. What else did the company have? A bunch of computers? Its inventory was always available to anyone who cared to look for it.

However, there had been reports that the team had got a raw deal and that only a few in the company had made money. But that was how it was always meant to be. Only about two dozen of the team had shares in the company. The rest did not, but they never had to make the sacrifices one has to in a start-up either. They drew good salaries. That is how the company was structured.

Phani, now restricted by rules laid down by Ibibo's media and public relations team, was not talking to anyone outside. But someone was, and was not projecting the true picture. There was chaos.

To the new owner, with its headquarters in Gurgaon, things seemed even worse. Did they end up with a guy who, having sold his company, did not care what happened to it? Ibibo's stinker came as no surprise to Phani: 'Boss, all hell is breaking loose and you are not even accessible.' Not their exact words, but along those lines.

It took a long time to calm things down. Yet, it cannot be said with certainty that the reputation of the redBus founders as nice and honest men was ever fully restored. The fact is, few in the redBus team had taken the risks the co-founders had taken to grow the company, nor even the risk that Sarika had taken in marrying a private bus ticketing agent. No one had asked why the co-founders were paid less than some of the managers they had hired, and why Phani was riding a motorbike when many in his team were driving big cars.

As Phani wonders aloud in his rented house in Bangalore's C.V. Raman Nagar, his infant son in his lap, his i10 parked downstairs, and Sarika apologizing for not giving me the lunch she had promised because she had to take her sick maid to the doctor, you want to join him in raising those questions.

~

In early February 2015, Kunal Bahl was sitting with another Kunal—Kunal Shah, co-founder of FreeCharge, a mobile recharge and coupon company—at Sahara Star, a hotel on the edge of Mumbai's domestic airport terminal. Rohit Bansal was also with them, as were Sandeep Tandon, Shah's co-founder at FreeCharge, and Alok Goel, their CEO.

Snapdeal and FreeCharge used to do business together. But this meeting was different. It was the result of a phone call Bahl had made to Shah to suggest that the two companies come together.

For Goel, it was a familiar feeling. He was the CEO of redBus when it was acquired by Naspers. He left redBus after that deal, and was lured by FreeCharge to become its CEO when founders Shah and Tandon parted with their personal equity to make the deal attractive for Goel.

The Snapdeal–FreeCharge deal generated none of the heat associated with the previous one. The two companies have not declared the size of the deal, but media reports suggest $400 million, most of it to be paid in the form of Snapdeal stock.

That makes it the largest deal in India's e-commerce segment. Yet, it took all of twenty-three days to seal the deal. There was no investment banker involved, only legal advisors. Soon after the meeting at Sahara Star, the FreeCharge leadership met their senior managers and told them they were in talks for a deal, but that there was no threat to anyone's job. The managers conveyed this to their teams. There were a dozen more meetings to keep the entire team of 180 informed about the progress of the deal.

From the beginning, Kunal Bahl had made it clear that FreeCharge would continue to work as an independent entity. That is Snapdeal's way of creating its own ecosystem. It started with making small acquisitions, but kept the 2014 M&A calendar busy with five: Doozton, a social product discovery technology platform; Wishpicker, a gift recommendation technology platform; Grabbon, a group buying site; eSportsBuy, an online sports goods retailer; and Shopo, an online marketplace for handicrafts. It went on to make bigger ones the next year: FreeCharge, RupeePower, and Exclusively.

'Our lens is consumption, not just retail,' says Kunal.

The centre of his universe is the user account, where consumers store cards, address details, etc. Around that is a family of marketplaces or different apps for buying. This structure allows one to buy all kinds of products on Snapdeal—some 15 million at the time Kunal and I met, not counting books, music and movies, which constitute the bulk of items, numbers-wise on most sites. Snapdeal had 40 million registered users and more than 100,000 merchants, the latter number slated to grow to a million in three years. It was adding a new product every ten seconds.

However, Snapdeal is not seen as the right platform for high fashion. For that, there is Exclusively.in. (You would remember it as the one Internet company in which Avnish Bajaj came close to losing money on his investment. But Myntra bought it. So Avnish got Myntra shares and ended up making money. After Flipkart bought Myntra, the founders of Exclusively.in bought the company back. They later sold it to Snapdeal.) It sells stuff from some of the country's top designers: Manish Malhotra, Tarun Tahiliani, Manish Arora, Anita Dongre, Rohit Bal, Gaurav Gupta, J.J. Valaya, Ritu Kumar and Varun Bahl.

FreeCharge takes care of utilities and other bill payments, recharging of phones and now, mobile wallets. RupeePower provides marketplace loans, credit cards, and financial services.

This is a family that will only grow. Most people see e-commerce as a percentage of retail. Kunal sees it as a percentage of consumption. Consumption is much bigger than retail. It includes travel, utility payments, education, financial services, etc.

'We make the supply chain for everything more efficient, we connect the dots between demand and supply more effectively. Why can't we now do it across different consumption spends? Why can't we make a large chunk of that go online for efficiency?'

Snapdeal is addressing a bunch of supply chain issues with its fulfilment programme for sellers. More than half of its orders are shipped through its fulfilment centres. It does not own a single piece of inventory, and never will. Sellers deposit their products at its fulfilment centres and Snapdeal ships them out. That reduces time to delivery and improves quality control and homogeneity of packaging. In a very short time, Snapdeal has built up a million square feet of space. By the end of 2015, it will have a cumulative three million square feet of space across fifty cities. Some of the big cities have more than one such centre. The space is rented out to sellers who do not have the resources to own their own space. The idea is to get close to the supply.

Then there is Snapdeal's investment in GoJavas, a third-party logistics company, for a significant but less-than-majority stake. Over the years, Snapdeal has been one of the largest customers of third-party logistics companies because it has never done the last mile itself. It did not want thousands of people on its rolls just to make deliveries.

However, it realized that one of the companies it worked with, GoJavas, was doing significantly better in service quality than the others. So it made sense to have it build focused capacity for Snapdeal.

'Our sales were growing faster than the capacity 3PLs (third-party logistics companies) were able to build. So we said we will invest in some of those companies. We did not want the problems every e-commerce company faced during Diwali last year: so much volume, but no one to deliver it.'

GoJavas provides additional value with delivery. The buyer can swipe a card with its delivery person, or open the box and see the product before paying. Its terms with Snapdeal allow it the freedom to work with other companies too.

Snapdeal has deliberately stayed out of two verticals. The first is furniture, which is gaining traction online but needs people with specific skills to install furniture at homes and fix them if repair is required. The second is grocery, which is already taken care of by the neighbourhood kirana stores.

'I don't know what problem we will be solving there.'

So, is problem-solving at the heart of his entrepreneurial philosophy?

'Solving a real need.'

Kunal believes everything done by Snapdeal so far has resulted in solving a real need. For instance, there are only four luxury malls in the country today. Maybe there will be five more in the next ten years. A person in Ludhiana who wants to buy something fancy will have to travel to Delhi or ask someone to get it for him from Delhi. He has the option now to buy it on Exclusively.in.

So, too, with RupeePower, which gave loans worth Rs 1500 crore in 2014–15 and was on track for Rs 3500 crore in 2015–16. That solves a real need in a country with few credit cards, where people in urgent need of money resort to personal loans, which are difficult to get and cost usurious rates of interest.

It is not just about the buyers. Snapdeal finances sellers, too, through its Capital Assist Programme. When I met Kunal in April 2015, nearly Rs 100 crore in loans had been given to small businesses on Snapdeal's platform, and none had gone bad. The borrowing business was paying interest rates

100–150 basis points cheaper than loans from other sources. What they save in interest costs, they pass on to the buyers of their goods, which in turn increases sales volumes.

Sales volumes grew almost 500 per cent in 2014–15. But there is more to this growth than just the numbers. Excluding the call centre operations, Snapdeal is a 3000-people company, much lighter staffed than its competitors are. And most of the people it is adding are in engineering, because it is trying to implement more automation and innovation. You build a much more valuable business if you can achieve growth with less resources than anyone else.

'The reason for that is our business model and culture. Inventory-led models, everywhere in the world, have always required far more capital to grow. Secondly, culture-wise, we are a frugal company. Look at our surroundings, they are pretty basic. This table was one of the cafeteria tables in the office. We just painted it blue and red.'

Blue and red are Snapdeal's colours.

~

In August 2015, as I toiled at my desk at the *Hindustan Times* in New Delhi, which I had joined the previous month, a press release arrived in my inbox. Quietly, unassumingly, the Shashank way.

Practo had raised $90 million from a bunch of investors led by Tencent, the Chinese Internet giant and fund house behind WeChat. The other investors were Sofina, Sequoia India, Google Capital, Altimeter Capital, Matrix Partners, Sequoia Capital Global Equities and Yuri Milner.

Practo, which had raised $30 million from Sequoia India and Matrix Partners a few months ago, had now raised a total of $125 million, which it claimed was one of the largest amounts raised in the world of digital health.

In the last six months, the press release said, Practo had grown six times to have 200,000 healthcare practitioners on its platform, and 10 million monthly searches by consumers looking for healthcare advice or treatment.

Practo.com had started only two years ago as a consumer-facing portal to find doctors. It is free for both doctors (to list) and patients (to find a doctor and book an appointment). It allows contextual advertisements from hospitals and clinics in demarcated sections of the website, similar to what Google does.

There are other revenue streams. The first and oldest is Practo Ray, which has basic and premium versions. The premium plan includes a cloud telephony-based IVR system for doctors.

In April, Practo had made its first acquisition, FitHo, which is in the wellness space. In July it made the second, an app and e-commerce development company. Qikwell and Insta Health were added soon after to the fold. Qikwell helps hospitals book appointments. Insta Health is a cloud-based hospital management software. Talks with two insurance companies are said to be going on for placement of their products on Practo.com. An ad revenue-based product like Google's, through which space can be sold to advertisers, is also said to be on the anvil.

All these acquisitions happened after Shashank and I met in March, when he was already saying the journey had been amazing for him. 'This is Phanindra telling you that entrepreneurship is self-purification. Your limitations can become magnified fast. If you are smart, you will identify your limitations and overcome them before it becomes a limitation to the company.'

An entrepreneur needs to be different people at different times: frugal, focused, dominating, survivor, manager, leader, visionary and communicator. A lot of learning and unlearning needs to be done. Every six to eight months, Shashank asks himself what he needs to change.

'A start-up is the best exposure you can get. It has been a big self-learning tool for me.'

The early years of bootstrapping—some of it not by choice—means that the founding team of Practo retains a chunk of equity that would be just shy of 50 per cent, which is something unusually healthy these days for a well-funded company. When well-funded, most companies see promoters' stakes dip to the single digits.

After all those years of rigour, Shashank has moved from binging on Red Bull to tucking into Thai food, for which he would happily walk a mile, without shoes.

'Red Bull to Thai food . . .'—he munched on that for a moment—'that's a good way to put it.'

What about sharing the journey with someone? How easy or difficult is it to find a life partner?

'Your social life gets affected because you don't have the time. Definitely, dating an entrepreneur is a nightmare you don't want to put anyone through.'

How about marrying an entrepreneur?

'Not a bad idea. There will be a far greater understanding of what the other is going through.'

Shashank was not married at the time we met. But whoever dated or married him would have a bit of work to do to understand him. He is, well, different—in a very nice and welcome way.

It worries him that our engineers are bought over like mercenaries. Young men and women should choose what they want to do, and it should be something they are passionate about, not just something that pays their bills or brings them a certain status.

'Everything,' he says, 'should be done with a purpose. Follow the purpose. It will take you through some tunnels, but it is the right truth. Entrepreneurs should build long-lasting businesses. That is what the world needs. It does not need flash-in-the-pan activities where one sees a brief spark of magic happen. We don't need magic. We need hard-working industrialists like the Tatas. You can make $100 million. What will you do with it? Imagine building an organization that outlasts you, one that lasts 100 years, 200 years. Won't that be surreal?'

What if someone made a really good offer to buy Practo?

This makes Shashank a little uncertain. 'I wouldn't know what to do with that money,' he says finally. 'I would probably put it in this business and run it. This is the most exciting thing I have done in my life. And this needs to be done. If not by me, then by somebody else. I am not doing it for the investor, I am doing it for myself. This has to get fixed. That's it. I don't care about anything else. If some other company can do it, I will be happy to share my thoughts with them. Let's just solve the goddamn problem.'

In spite of his youth, Shashank is approached by many aspiring entrepreneurs for advice. Some are even younger than him, and some come to him because he is sort of a pioneer.

Many of the advice seekers say: 'Shashank, I cannot continue at what I am doing because I have not been able to make money.'

'Wrong business model,' says Shashank. 'First tell me, why did you start?'

They should not have started because they wanted money. 'Just start,' is Shashank's advice. If they are doing the right thing, money will follow. 'Don't start because you can raise money. Start because you believe in something, want to change something. If you can look into the mirror and say you are going to do this whether someone pays you or not, that you can do it in spite of the suffering, then start your company.'

But, isn't fundraising the name of the game now?

'Money is a differentiator. It accelerates things. But it cannot replace innovation, which is the base. Without the base, you are all talk and no walk. During tough times, it is innovation that comes to your rescue, not the money in the bank.'

Are tough times coming?

'Tough times will come—in two years, three years, four years . . . they will come. The important question is, how many downturns can you take? The downturn will remove the chaff from the wheat. You are making commitments to your team, the team's families and their future. Do you have a sound base? Tomorrow, if the money dries up, do you have what it takes to be around?'

Red Bull, perhaps?

~

Kunal met Yashna, who runs a company that sells flavoured candy floss, for the first time on 17 December 2011, a few days after he told the Snapdeal board he had shut down the deals business to start an online marketplace. They got married four months later.

Yashna has had a ringside view of Snapdeal's journey, with all its twists and turns. She now uses the 2006 model of the Honda Civic Kunal had bought second-hand in 2008. He sees no point in buying a new vehicle, since cars lose value fast as soon as driven out of the showroom.

'When you get married, you realize your wife also needs a car. I tried to get her to share a car with other people, but it was not working out,' says Kunal. He was now forced to buy another car, a Toyota Camry Hybrid. This, too, was owned by someone else before. He has never owned a watch.

In that sense, Kunal and his approach to life have not changed much, other than his having a higher sense of financial security. No one in Snapdeal flies business class. When Kunal and Rohit go to Bangalore, they stay in the same service apartment where they stayed during their visits to the city to sign up companies for the deals business.

'I am a low-maintenance guy high on experience.' So he travels a lot. He tries to watch two movies every weekend, though often it is just one because there isn't another worth watching.

There was a time when he really wanted to teach, and even went to the extent of meeting the principal of DPS R.K. Puram, where he had studied.

It was a meeting that he managed after a lot of following up. Kunal told the principal about his background, that he was passionate about technology entrepreneurship, what it could do for India, and that our system of education did not do anything to support it. He said he would love to come in once a week and teach a course on entrepreneurship. Students from any class could attend. After all, entrepreneurship has no age; you can be an entrepreneur at ten. The class would talk about technology entrepreneurship, watch videos, discuss examples and business models, and follow Internet and mobile growth.

The principal told Kunal to come back the next year, that the school's session had started and he could not accommodate him in the middle of it. Kunal called him two months later. 'Have you changed your mind?'

He hadn't. 'I told you to come next year.'

As a last ditch attempt, Kunal said he could organize a fundraising programme for the school. But the principal was not impressed. He said: *'Bhagwan ki daya se bahut paisa hai hamare paas.'*

Kunal did not call again. Imagine the lessons he might have taught to a whole generation.

～

CHAPTER 9

An afternoon meeting with a stranger at a common friend's office in Jhandewalan—a Delhi locality that has appeared in countless photos and movies because of its gigantic Hanuman statue that constantly peers over the passing metro trains—turned out to be serendipitous for Manmohan Agarwal. This stranger, Nitin, his friend's friend, had the same surname as he did. Anyway, it is a surname to which every tenth man in Jhandewalan and the neighbouring Karol Bagh would likely answer to.

Manmohan was excited because Nitin echoed his own thoughts about the future of e-commerce in India. It was evening. Their common friend, who was now sulking at being left out of the conversation, wanted to close down the shutters of his office. Manmohan suggested they move to Panchsheel Club and continue their conversation. Nitin agreed, and the two Agarwals drank and chatted till 3 a.m.

Seven hours later, they spoke on the phone and decided to do it.

'It' was Bigshoebazaar, an online venture to sell shoes.

Manmohan had recently left Vishal Retail, where, as COO, he had seen the best of times—growing it from 500,000 square feet to 3 million square feet in eighteen months, making it the only pan-India retail chain, with stores from Udhampur to Dimapur and from Kochi to Agartala—and the worst of times, when Vishal collapsed and was eventually sold to the private equity giant, TPG Capital.

Vishal Retail, focused on the bottom of the pyramid, seemed like the perfect model for India—it appeared to be the real Walmart of India. The company, in following the consumption-led retail story unfolding in India, overlooked the fact that the industry in India was terribly fragmented too. Purchasing power varied sharply across the country—from state to state, city to city, and even from locality to locality within cities. It was easy to open Vishal stores in small cities, but it was difficult to turn a profit from them in spite of the high footfalls.

There would be no such problems with e-commerce. The online platform would draw in those customers who had the money and the desire to buy, wherever they were. Geography was going to be history. 'What we need to crack is the supply chain,' Manmohan told Nitin.

'I will get Rajul,' said Nitin.

Rajul Jain had been Nitin's classmate at IIT Delhi, and had earned a formidable reputation for handling operations after graduating from the institute. There was also Danish Ahmed, the youngest of the four, the original founder of Bigshoebazaar.com. He was in his mid-twenties and found himself out of breath running the company. Manmohan, thirty-eight, and Nitin, thirty-four, had a wealth of start-up experience behind them, and the company would do well to have them as co-founders.

Within forty-eight hours, they were all on board.

The speed was in keeping with the times. E-retail was already flourishing in Brazil and Russia—both economies comparable with India—as noted by Goldman Sachs's BRIC report. It had been tried in India for years, mainly by Indiatimes and Rediff, but had never really taken off.

Manmohan, Nitin, Rajul, and Danish were out to show how e-retail ought to be done.

They had company in Sachin Bansal and Binny Bansal of Flipkart, Kunal Bahl of Snapdeal, and Pearl Uppal of FashionAndYou. These companies became the four beacons of the future of e-commerce in India. However, only two of them continue to glow.

Flipkart created the first real buzz, with $10 million in Series B funding from Tiger Global in 2010, and stirred things up further with $20 million the following year, again from Tiger. Flipkart sold only books when it started, and went on to sell everything else shortly after. FashionAndYou, in keeping with its name, focused on fashion, and Snapdeal on coupons.

Bigshoebazaar carved out its own space. The shoe site was up and running in September 2009. In the beginning, it had a hard time convincing brands to come on board. 'What is the point?' the brand guys said. 'Nobody will buy shoes without first trying them on.' Normally, customers walk a few paces wearing their new shoes before buying them. 'You will be back in six months to return the stock.'

Bigshoebazaar was not back in six months. Shoes would go on to become one of the biggest surprises in online retail in India. Bigshoebazaar rode the wave, even managing to convince several brands to shell out the usual retail margin of 35–40 per cent. Initially, the brands wanted to give no more than 5–10 per cent. 'You have no costs,' they said, until Manmohan and his co-founders demonstrated to them that online retail had just as much costs as offline.

The team did not want to coast on simply shoes.

Bigshoebazaar's initial capital had come from the three Fs of start-up funding: friends, family, and fools. Manmohan and the other co-founders met many VCs, who did not think India was ready for e-commerce yet. Credit cards had yet to proliferate. Processing online payments was an ordeal. Logistics were nascent. Then, as sentiment turned, Nexus Venture Partners, a US- and India-based fund, pumped in $2 million in 2010. This money fuelled ambition, and Bigshoebazaar would soon pivot on that funding to become yebhi.com in early 2011, expanding its range to include apparel.

It was a natural progression. Nearly all the shoe companies—the likes of Nike, Reebok and Woodland, were already into apparel. The reverse was happening, too, with apparel brands like Louis Philippe, Numero Uno and Van Heusen now selling shoes.

Things were looking up. Within six months of entering the space, Yebhi became the largest online apparel retailer in India. Global investors were now getting in touch, to understand what the hell was going on in e-commerce in India.

Everyone raised money around this time. Snapdeal and FashionAndYou raised Rs 200 crore each in 2011. Flipkart, by now the clear trailblazer, raised about twice as much. But Yebhi got the best quality money, from N.R. Narayana Murthy's family investment vehicle, Catamaran. There was a Silicon Valley investor who wanted to invest in the company in Series B, but Manmohan plumped for Catamaran. In the space of Internet, technology, and start-ups, Murthy's name carried more weight than valley dollars. The only problem was that this money from a pedigreed source was less than the amounts Flipkart, Snapdeal and even FashionAndYou had managed to raise. Yebhi raised only Rs 40 crore.

Yebhi thirsted for more. With the Series A funding from Nexus six months ago, Yebhi had grown six times. Now it needed big money, at least Rs 75 crore or so. But the investors wanted to see more 'traction'—a word fund-starved start-ups have come to dread—before committing to more. When investors refer to traction, they mean they want to see evidence in the marketplace that the goods or services offered by the start-up are increasing in value. It was a catch-22; the traction would not come without more capital.

~

Harish Bahl wears his entrepreneurship on his sleeve. He stops me cheerfully as I try to make space for his coffee cup at our tiny table in the American Diner at New Delhi's India Habitat Centre. 'Entrepreneur *aadmi hain yaar, kahin bhi pee lenge.*' (I'm an entrepreneur, dude, I'll manage.)

That's the way Harish is: cheerful even when making a point, which he does with an easy and friendly smattering of Delhi–Hindi. That, and his medium height, medium build, and dark hair, make him look younger than his forty-two years.

Being an entrepreneur, he believes, is a lifestyle decision rather than a commercial one. If one is successful, one ends up making money, too. But people who start with a commercial motive often end up on the losing side. If it was an arithmetical decision, all analysts would be entrepreneurs, and they would all be very rich.

At the same time, entrepreneurship also needs the analyst's rigour. 'I have come across so many people who claim to be entrepreneurs and are perceived to be entrepreneurs, too, but in reality are not entrepreneurs at all. Entrepreneurship is not about indiscipline, enjoyment or perks.'

There are perks, surely—one of them being your own boss?

Harish would hear none of it. 'What the hell does that mean? I have not taken more than five days of leave in the last ten years. I push myself even if I am running a 101-degree fever. Is that being your own boss, or being super-disciplined? A good entrepreneur would be the first in and last out of the office. On the other hand, in an MNC, if you are the most senior guy, you would generally be the last in, first out.'

Harish chose to become an entrepreneur upon graduating from the SDM College of Engineering and Technology in Dharwad, Karnataka. His father had a small auto parts business in Bhogal, near New Delhi's Nizamuddin area. Harish started making bulletproof cars. Three years later, he was bored.

This was the late 1990s. 'Internet', 'digital' and 'dotcom' were the buzzwords. So Harish set up the Smile Group in 1999, which would incubate—at a time when the word incubate was used more in poultry farms than in corporate circles—Internet start-ups.

Smile started small in revenue and scale, but not in ambition. The day Harish had his first Rs 1.5 lakh in the bank, he went to Silicon Valley in the United States to see how start-up investments were done there. With hundreds of start-ups sprouting there, the valley was, to an aspiring entrepreneur, what a wholesale market is to a small trader. 'I thought *mandi toh udhar hi hai na, pehle mandi mein jaa kar dekhte hain bikta kya hai.*' (I thought I should check out the Valley market to see what is sold there.) Harish had a friend there, so he was not worried about the cost of staying.

This was 2000–01. Once there, Harish stumbled on to something that tickled his curiosity: a job fair. *'Ye mela kyun lagate hain naukri dene ke liye, hamare desh mein to sifarish lagate hain.'* (Those people were putting up a job fair, while back home you have to get someone to put in a word for you to get a job.)

Harish visited the fair. His computer science degree from Dharwad landed him a job that would pay him much more than Smile's entire turnover. Smile was a web development agency at the time. Out of excitement, Harish called his father and told him about the job. He was excited that someone thought he was worth so much money. 'Don't come back, get your visa changed,' said his father.

But Harish told him he was booked on a flight back to India after four days, and he was taking the flight. 'Are you coming to get your things?' asked his father.

'No,' said Harish, 'I am coming back to run my own company. Hundreds of Americans will one day work for me.'

His father did not speak to him for a month after his return. He had worked hard to get Harish an education, and now Harish had thrown away a glorious opportunity. For the next few years, as the tech bubble burst, Harish was reminded of his father's words every day. All his friends said he had done the wrong thing.

Now they say he did the right thing. He has had partnerships with Airbnb, WPP Digital, Ogilvy and Yahoo. Smile Group has given birth to, and nurtured, several companies like online jewellery seller, Juvalia, and lifestyle brand, Freecultr.

It has also had two failures. BeStylish started as a footwear e-tailer—India's Zappos—later becoming a marketplace, and then an aggregator for others like Myntra, Jabong and Flipkart, but not meeting with success in any form. DealsandYou was a group buying site. Last heard, Bahl was trying to change its business model.

Then there is FashionAndYou, started in 2009 as a flash sale site modelled on Vipshop, China's largest discount sales site.

~

'Diwali of 2014 will be the inflection point for e-commerce in India,' Manmohan was telling the Yebhi board, his co-founders, and any investor who would care to listen. This was 2012, and a bonanza from the festival season two years later appeared to be a distant dream to most people. They could not foresee the online user base, at 4 million then, jumping to 20 million in just two years. Manmohan spoke ad-infinitum about consumer sentiment, which he thought was clearly turning. But they wouldn't listen. They listened even less after the LetsBuy story.

LetsBuy's is a curious story. It was started in 2009 by Hitesh Dhingra, who had earlier co-founded Tyroo, an online advertising network. It raised $6 million in January 2011 from Helion Venture Partners, Accel Partners and Tiger Global. A year later it was acquired by Flipkart. It shut shop in May 2012, redirecting its considerable traffic to Flipkart.

Curiously, Helion, Accel and Tiger are also the main investors in Flipkart. The subsuming of LetsBuy into Flipkart raised several questions about conflicts of interest in the funding and running of online retail firms. This considerably weakened investor belief in India's e-commerce story. Some of these investors were the investors in Yebhi.

Yebhi raised another Rs 100 crore in 2012, but this amount was only half of its real requirement. It ran out of money before the year was over.

'Just six more months,' Manmohan thought wistfully. Six more months of capital, and Yebhi could have been a different story. It could have flown into the stratosphere, just like Flipkart and Snapdeal.

By now, the political climate in the country had changed drastically. There was a UPA corruption scandal erupting every week, and 'policy paralysis' had become a commonly used phrase. Everyone was now looking ahead to the elections.

Yebhi's investors would not listen to Manmohan's entreaties of 'just one more year; we have done all the hard work'. They weren't willing to stay for a single day longer.

'You are on your own,' they told Manmohan and the others in September 2013, leaving them with unfulfilled ambitions and Rs 25 crore in liabilities. Some of the liabilities were taken care of by selling assets and inventory. Four months later, in January 2014, Rajul left to join Myntra as head of supply chain. Nitin quit to join Equirus, a boutique investment bank.

Incredibly, Yebhi changed its avatar again. Danish Ahmed, the original founder of Bigshoebazaar, which had become Yebhi, is now CEO as the company becomes an O2O—online-to-offline—outfit. Its website tells visitors where the stocks and discounts are in offline retail. In its pomp, Yebhi had 1400 employees. It now has thirty. In 2012, it had a 50,000 square-foot office. That has shrunk to 1200 square feet.

Manmohan, who was the CEO at Yebhi, has become the managing director now, and is simultaneously trying to start another online venture. He has not changed much physically. His hair and thin moustache appear black without the benefit of colouring. Maybe he can withstand the stress better because his wife is a constant source of support. They had met as students in Allahabad—she was in class twelve and he, five years her senior, was graduating. Ever since, they have remained best friends; there is nothing on Manmohan's mind that he does not tell his wife.

But does he have anything to tell Nitin these days? The answer is a contrast to that day of torrential conversation in Jhandewalan and their night of drinks and dreams in Panchsheel Club.

'I can pick up the phone and talk to him if I need to, but we don't really have much to talk about.'

Would he call Nitin, the investment banker, to raise funds for a new venture?

'No.'

~

Pearl Uppal had the first of her two sons in December 2007, when she was thirty-two. She had been with Yahoo India for five years and had risen to head all monetization—anything that could generate revenue. She had 120 people reporting to her.

It was a great job, but Pearl was not sure where she would go from there. She was not sure where Yahoo would go from there. Google was growing, and Yahoo was stagnating. Now that she was a mother, she also wanted a little work-life balance.

So she decided to turn entrepreneur. She thought it would allow her to create her own schedule. 'I realized only later, much to my surprise, that there is no work-life balance for an entrepreneur,' she says with a chuckle.

We meet over coffee and cookies in Gurgaon, at the far corner table of a restaurant in a hotel. Pearl is so slim she looks younger than her forty years. She speaks in an animated manner, her expressions complementing the rise and fall of her voice.

She is busier than ever these days. She runs TalkingThreads.com, a site for specialized fabric and clothing, with her mother, and a fund called Startup Superfuel with her husband. She is in no hurry to grow TalkingThreads. She does not want a repeat of the breakneck pace she kept up at her first start-up, FashionAndYou, one of the brightest early stars in India's e-commerce. And as a provider of early stage money to young start-ups at Superfuel, she is careful not to allow herself to slip into the kind of situation she had to face at FashionAndYou.

FashionAndYou just happened to Pearl. In spite of her yearning for more time with her child, she was open to signing up for a new job, mainly because she had no clue how one went about setting up a company. She did not know many entrepreneurs. There were anyway not many entrepreneurs around at the time.

When Harish Bahl called, Pearl had been studying business models of fashion companies, purely out of interest.

She had always been interested in the area, and admired fashion brands and retailers. The years at Yahoo, and before that a couple at Rediff, had given her a grounding in Internet-related matters. She read about the Gilt Groupe in *Time* magazine. It was one of the buzziest start-ups in New York. Starting in 2007, Gilt relied on flash sales, which consisted in selling luxury designer items at deep discounts over short bursts of time. These sales were frequent—several times on certain days.

Something told Pearl the model would work in India. She vaguely knew about Harish Bahl and his Smile Group; Harish Bahl had met her in the corporate circuit. Harish had called because he had heard Pearl was looking for a change.

'What are you doing these days?' he asked.

'Not much,' she said. 'Wondering whether to build a business of my own or take up a job.'

They met over coffee. The Smile Group was incubating a number of start-ups in various areas, including fashion, with money from overseas investors.

'I would like to do a gilt.com kind of thing,' said Pearl. She was convinced there was a large, untapped market in fashion retail.

It was the right fit. Harish got a co-founder, the term used for those who executed Smile's projects. They would get two other co-founders. Harish would be the founder.

'I'll do it,' she said.

They shook hands. Pearl left Yahoo and started FashionAndYou in November 2009 as the CEO and co-founder. Harish got a couple of German investors to bring in the money.

Pearl did not even get into the details of the shareholding structure. She ought to have.

~

If Nitin Agarwal were to do Yebhi all over again, he would do it pretty much the same way. He would do it with a different team, that's all.

In early 2009, Nitin was taking his own sweet time to figure out what to do with his life. He had just become free from Brain Visa, the e-learning services company he had started in 2000 with Supam Maheshwari and Vikas Kumar. They had sold it in 2007 for $30 million and gone their separate ways, though both Supam and Vikas remained close friends with Nitin, especially Supam, who set up a joint investment kitty with Nitin. The two still speak nearly every day, but Supam hardly ever talks about the fund. Nitin manages it. When they were at Brain Visa, Nitin's shares were with Supam for safekeeping.

That degree of trust was missing among the Yebhi co-founders.

Danish's Bigshoebazaar tempted Nitin. The idea of e-commerce held an irresistible appeal for Nitin. He had been exposed to it on his several visits to the United States to meet Brain Visa clients. Surely, the damn thing deserved another chance in India. Its story could not possibly end with Indiatimes and Rediff. All it needed was consumer trust.

Danish was a bright chap, and the idea of selling shoes online held immense promise. Zappos had pulled it off in the West. Bigshoebazaar could be India's Zappos. But not with the team Danish had put together. Nitin had already given him word that he would invest in the company, but told him the team was not a great one. Something had to be done. If Nitin was to go so deep into Bigshoebazaar so as to fiddle with its team, why would he stop at being just an investor?

Manmohan Agarwal had seemed okay the day they first met in Jhandewalan. More importantly, he was the kind of guy Nitin had been advised to take on board. His retail experience was rich, even if Vishal had been snuffed out.

'Let's recapitalize and do it as a co-venture. I wanted to do e-commerce anyway.'

Danish was delighted.

After Brain Visa's success, Rajul had often told Nitin: 'Let me know if there is a place for me in your next venture.'

Initially, things went swimmingly well. There was joy in the air as the four of them dreamed of making it big, and everything seemed well on course.

In the beginning, Nitin was the only one among the co-founders to put in his money into Bigshoebazaar, which was fine, as he was the only one who had the money to invest. He and some friends of his put in the seed capital of Rs 2 crore. In return, he was given a bigger chunk of equity than the other three co-founders.

The co-founders carved up the responsibility nicely, based on their expertise. Nitin took care of technology, marketing, and setting-up processes. Rajul was looking after operations: warehouse, logistics, call centre. Danish was in sourcing. Manmohan took charge of finance, sourcing and administration.

They needed to pick a CEO from among themselves. 'You are the oldest and the most experienced. You become the CEO,' Nitin told Manmohan.

As Brain Visa had taught Nitin, these things did not matter much.

Now he was to learn a different lesson.

There were the usual differences of opinion every set of co-founders faces in a start-up. At Brain Visa, Nitin had endless discussions with Supam and Vikas, with each voice being exactly equal to the other. At times the discussions lasted days and nights.

In Yebhi, the discussions ended quickly because Manmohan flashed his CEO card.

Why didn't Nitin flash his largest-shareholder card? Well, then matters would have come to a head and probably reached a point of no return. In 2011, as Yebhi was soaring, it seemed like a foolish thing to do. The wise thing to do was to build the company together, which was why they had joined hands in the first place.

They differed bitterly over the choice of investor and the size of investment.

Manmohan wanted to wait for the right investor and was willing to turn money down from a large investor. Nitin could not believe his ears. He understood the value of opportunity and the cost of a lost one. If Yebhi did not get into bed with this e-commerce MNC, the MNC would find someone else, and that someone else would have the capital to become big and kill Yebhi.

'He can be either on your side or on the other side. What do you want?' Nitin asked Manmohan. But Manmohan just did not get it. Today, the large fund and the e-commerce MNC run a large e-commerce outfit in India, one that is thriving.

By now, Nitin had had enough. He told Manmohan he wanted to quit, only to be persuaded to stay. To be honest, he did not need that much persuasion, since the Yebhi dream had not quite died in his eyes.

For some time, Nitin thought the investors would give Yebhi a little more rope. There was a bridge round of funding of Rs 30 crore in early 2013. But, as bridge rounds go, that was it. The investors exited in September that year. Nitin left in January 2014 to join Equirus, which allows him to work pretty much as an entrepreneur, with his own profit and loss account. He got over Yebhi.

But there are still nights when two thoughts keep him awake. One is about what could have been. Yebhi could have stood toe to toe with Flipkart today, its valuation soaring just as high. The other thought is about what his next start-up venture can be.

From time to time, Nitin's voice falls to a whisper or rises loud enough to be heard over the ruckus a bunch of elderly men are creating at the next table at Cafe Coffee Day in New Delhi's GK II. Like many of the other entrepreneurs, Nitin. too, with his thin, clean-shaven face, looks younger than his thirty-eight years.

He points out that he is younger than Jack Ma was when he started Alibaba.

~

In 2012, Harish Bahl spoke to Kotak Mahindra Bank for a loan. The bank asked for collateral. Harish offered his house in Lajpat Nagar, New Delhi, one of the two houses he owned in the city. The house was still mortgaged when we met, but the loan raised against it helped save FashionAndYou, which was on the verge of shutting down.

Why didn't he simply shut it down?

Two reasons. The first was his belief in FashionAndYou and its model of flash sales. The only problem was its being a little ahead of its time, coming as it did before Jabong and Myntra, both of which now dominate online retail in fashion.

FashionAndYou offered big discounts on big brands, but for a short period of time. For that it needed a big surplus stock with big brands. But in India, the luxury fashion market was small. 'If you look at, say, Ralph Lauren,' says Harish, pointing to the little horse on my jacket, 'you don't get it in India. The one I am wearing, what is it . . . '

He asks me to read the label at the back of his neck: Brooks Brothers.

'Brooks Brothers won't have more than three stores here. How much surplus inventory can you churn out with three

stores? Compare that with what a Macy's will churn out in
the US. Brooks Brothers would have a thousand stores in the
US. Imagine the surplus.'

So FashionAndYou grew rapidly early on, and raised
substantial funding. But soon its growth slowed down. That
is the way of all such outfits: Gilt in the US, QPVIP in Russia
and Marcopony in Turkey.

That is also what happened to several other start-ups in
very different areas. MakeMyTrip started well, shrank, then
expanded again. Its founder, Deep Kalra, never gave up;
he fought to keep it going through the lean period. Myntra
existed much before FashionAndYou. It used to make mugs
and T-shirts. Its founder, Mukesh Bansal, steered it through
different stages of difficulty, never giving up.

Exiting is an option more likely to be taken by 'hired
entrepreneurs'.

Now, who are those?

Harish dithers.

'Globally, 90 per cent of the successful entrepreneurs
started their businesses before they were thirty. I don't know
the exact reasons, but I know the statistics. You have to start
young. It has to be passion rather than pedigree. It has to be
your baby, not a dream sold to you by someone else.'

This is curious. Smile Group is a start-up incubator.
It partners with investors on one side and entrepreneurs
on the other, and brings them together on an idea that
appeals to both. In many cases, the entrepreneurs—they can
be three or four and are called co-founders—have only a
small percentage of equity in the incubated company and
work more like equity-holding professionals than as true
entrepreneurs.

Harish himself plays different roles at different stages of a
start-up. In the first stage, which he calls the sprint, Harish is
an active entrepreneurial partner with the co-founders. This is

a frenetic period of getting the idea validated, raising money from a VC, setting up the team, getting journalists to write about you, and growing rapidly month on month. Harish is totally sucked into the venture at this stage, but perhaps more focused on what not to do, 'because I have screwed up more in life'.

Once the venture has raised money, a board is set up and one of the co-founders is made the CEO. Harish is more like the executive chairman at this stage. Success or failure is now the co-founders' responsibility.

Things change after the second round of funding, or Series B. Harish limits his role in the start-up. He does resources (human, capital, infrastructure), arranges for the office, makes presentations before VCs, and does the big recruitments. He is an active board member though, doing weekly calls and monthly meetings with the team. He moves the needle on initiatives that will change the fortunes of the businesses: a feature that pivots the business or a new business line itself. He also does crisis management.

FashionAndYou is the one venture where he continues to play all these roles. He had addressed its supply constraints so that a large percentage of the stuff at the store does not consist of big brands, but of sarees, kurtis, shawls and lehengas. There may be dearth of inventory for Ralph Lauren jackets, but any number of sarees can be picked up from Surat and any number of shawls from Kashmir. And he mortgaged his house to put money into it.

'Everything was falling apart for Smile in 2012. Today, by God's grace, FashionAndYou is on a comeback, Freecultr is doing amazing well, and Tyroo is a market leader. The Africa business is a market leader. We are decent shareholders in Airbnb, which has become a $15 billion company; we have a joint venture with TPG. In one year so much crashed and in two years so much came back.'

That is why Harish never fears failure. Businesses can fail, but he has never for a moment felt he could himself fail. 'Entrepreneurs are not the most talented guys. I will never claim to be more intelligent than you. But they are more committed and have higher perseverance.' In his experience, these qualities arise from passion, and passion itself comes with being young. Harish explains it with two scenarios.

In the first, a young Suveen Sinha tells Harish Bahl about the digital news revolution. There is an opportunity to disrupt the Times Group and build a mobile base—a new, disruptive news destination.

'Let's do it,' says Suveen.

'Yes, man, I have also been thinking about it. Let's do it,' says Harish.

Both are passionate about it. Both are twenty-six. They have no clue how it will be done. They know nobody in the media world, have no money, haven't a clue how the media works, but are mad about it. And they are smart guys.

The chances of this venture succeeding are very high.

In the second scenario, Harish Bahl of Smile Group talks to the executive editor of *Business Today*.

'Hey Suveen, let's do it. I have this VC ready to give us $5 million. This is the idea. If you join, I will give you 10 per cent. In five years, that will be worth $100 million. You are the guy who has been there and done it.'

'Yeah, I know everybody,' says Suveen.

There is a very small chance this venture will succeed.

Start-up businesses are like sine waves. They move from crest to trough to crest to trough. The persons in the second scenario will enjoy the crests: the press conferences, announcements, coverage in print and on television, hiring people. But one day shit will hit the roof. No one will pay for the content. People will start to leave. Cash will begin to run out. Investors will say: 'Fuck you, you wasted my money.' For good measure, they will be banging the desk in the boardroom as they say 'screw you'. Journalists will call to ask where the hell the company is going.

The *Business Today* executive editor will say, 'Yaar, Harish, I don't think this is working out. I got a call yesterday from *Times*. They are offering me a good job.'

In his place, the Suveen of twenty-six, the one in the first scenario, will fight like a mongrel. He will try to reinvent, find a new way to do his business. He will challenge the unknown and find a way out. Because that is where he belongs, he does not know any alternative.

'It is passion versus pedigree,' says Harish. 'It is not about the $100 million. He wants to change India.'

Harish has gone through these phases. 'Every time, I was like, this is what I have to do. That, to me, is the underlying core of an entrepreneur's life. I have not seen an entrepreneur who has not locked himself up in the toilet and cried.'

Has he done that himself?

'Yes, I have, several times.'

That has taught him enough to console those who cry on his shoulders.

Three days before Harish and I met, he was driving one of his co-founders round and round the same loop of the road in Udyog Vihar, Gurgaon, late at night. The co-founder was weeping: 'What man, what life is this . . . '

The next two days were better. The company made notable progress. The man's spirits were back. And he came to knock on Harish's door. '*Chal, daru peene chalte hain.*' (Let's go grab a drink.)

Hired founders—those who are, in fact, glorified employees with a little bit of equity, who are in it for the money and glamour, the executive editor type—will be unable to ride the sine wave of crests and troughs. Devoid of the genuine entrepreneur's passion and ambition to change

the world, they will curse themselves every day for having left
their jobs. That will weaken them, drain them of the energy
to fight, kill creativity and innovation, and minimize their
chances of success.

There is this friend of Harish's, who used to be with
a Fortune 500 company, but left to start his own. He had a
calculated approach. He wanted to make a certain amount of
money by a certain time. One day Harish found him kicking the
wall. 'Bittu, what happened?' asked Harish, who wouldn't tell
me the friend's real name, for he is a well-known fellow. Bittu
ranted: 'I was a senior VP. I had a fucking secretary. Everything
was taken care of. What am I doing here? I have been trying for
two hours to book a ticket on IRCTC and it is not happening.'

There was more. 'My brother is coming from Nepal and
he wants me to pick him up from the airport. His wife has
given me things to do. They think I am sitting fucking *vela* out
here. My clients are not taking my calls. What is this rubbish?'

'Buddy,' Haris said, 'you *were* a senior VP. Today you
are part of a three-man company. Your company has zero
turnover. You have to do everything yourself.'

In Bittu's mind, the lifestyle decision was a raw deal.

To Harish's, it was never an issue. The other day he had
to make a quick trip, which would have taken a long time in
his Range Rover in Gurgaon's traffic. So Harish borrowed an
office boy's Bajaj Chetak. The office boy was amazed. 'Boss,
aap toh Range Rover *chalate hain.*'

'*Saley, woh toh abhi liya hai,*' Harish shot back. '*Zindagi
ke bees saal toh bitaye hain scooter par dhakke kha kar.*' (I
have spent twenty years of my life on a scooter, being pushed
around.)

The other day, Harish saw Sanjeev Bikhchandani in a
Honda Accord. The founder of Naukri.com and an investor
in highly valued companies like Zomato, Bikhchandani might
be worth a lot. But he is happy with an Accord.

'If you are an entrepreneur, and if you are honest to yourself, it is a super sexy life. I don't think I can do anything else. But if you are not an entrepreneur, you are going to regret every day of this journey.'

How was his rapport with the FashionAndYou co-founder, Pearl Uppal? During the bad times, did he shore up her confidence the way he did for the other guy driving around Udyog Vihar?

The question finds Harish evasive and dithering. It is all in the past.

'Today we have Vipshop as a shareholder in FashionAndYou. Vip is a world leader in flash sales. The fact that Vip came and invested says we have turned around.'

Was there a clash between FashionAndYou and BeStylish?

'There are two failures to my name, BeStylish and DealsandYou. I don't feel very bad about them. I feel bad that some money was lost. DealsandYou was not the only company to fail. There were seventeen funded companies in group buying. None succeeded. We returned the capital to our investors. We made an announcement when we raised money for DealsandYou, but not when we returned it. What had been spent had been spent. As for the rest of the money, we told the investors it was not working—either we pivot or return the capital. They asked for the capital to be returned. It was the same story with BeStylish. It was single category retail, ahead of its time. In 2012, Indian e-commerce was untouchable. There was no investment happening.'

But was there a clash between the two lifestyle outfits? 'If there was money lying in FashionAndYou, which was well funded, I could not have used it for BeStylish. They had different shareholders.'

~

Norwest Venture Partners, Intel Capital, Nokia Growth Partners, and Sequoia Capital together invested $40 million in FashionAndYou in October 2011, making it one of the most well-funded start-ups in India. It had a staff of almost 500, and worked with high fashion and luxury brands across apparel, designer wear, footwear, watches, jewellery, fragrances, etc., to sell their stuff at discounts of up to 80 per cent.

That was also the high-water mark for Pearl at the company, and her last hurrah. She left FashionAndYou eleven months after this.

Harish and Pearl were both reluctant to talk about what led to her exit, and when they did speak about it, they did not want to have it written about. Here is what I can say without, I hope, making either feel I am betraying their trust.

They are both sound, pedigreed professionals, but not quite made for each other as business partners. When the going got tough, as it invariably does with start-ups, neither thought of the other as the perfect ally.

The early phase of FashionAndYou was heady. Pearl put her shoulder to the wheel and rustled up a good team. She brought in people from retail, logistics, and merchandizing, and trained them in technology and the Internet. Her flash sale model clicked with consumers and investors. During this phase, Harish was right by her side, providing all the support she needed. It may have comforted her that her husband Gaurav Kachru joined Smile Group in February 2010 as group executive vice president of corporate development and strategy, and went on to helm one of its other start-ups, DealsandYou, as a co-founder and CEO.

Pearl loved the euphoria of building something path-breaking and seeing it attain traction and scale. But the flash sale is a model that plateaus sooner rather than later. This is what happened to Gilt, too. It ran out of steam and had to be resurrected, but never again reached the high points it had in its early phase.

FashionAndYou plateaued even faster. India did not have too many luxury and fashion labels at the time. Whatever stock was there, only 20 to 30 per cent of it would be available for discounts. Pearl wanted to pivot, not entirely giving up the flash sale model, but adding catalogue retail and full-priced items alongside.

Around this time, Myntra, which used to be derided by the FashionAndYou people as a T-shirt and coffee mug maker, was moving into catalogue retail and full-priced items, and gaining scale. Jabong was moving in too.

FashionAndYou could not execute a pivot as Pearl could not convince the bosses. And that, she thinks, is because her equity holding in the company was too small. Pearl and the two other co-founders of FashionAndYou shared the 30 per cent equity meant for them. Their individual portions shrank fast as funding came in. It did not matter much now whether they attended the board meetings or not.

'When you build something that you truly call your own, it has to reflect in the shareholding. Otherwise your voice matters only to the team reporting to you, not to the investors.'

She watched in helpless silence as FashionAndYou's growth tapered even as the rest of the e-commerce sector in India, including companies like Myntra and Jabong, surged with the tide.

The point arrived when she could watch on no more. What she needed to do was radical, breathless execution. But she found herself tied up in knot-ridden chains of approvals and clearances, and felt more like an executive reporting to a chairman and a board rather than an intrepid entrepreneur.

'This structure of entrepreneurship is faulty. The joy of entrepreneurship is not in the money you make, it is in being able to build a business. If you had to be just a CEO or a senior executive, you would rather be that in a big company and enjoy the perks. You don't want to be in entrepreneurship hell.'

She could not let her team see her powerlessness as it would dishearten them. But she did not have much sway left over the company, mainly because her equity holding was down to 3 per cent. She left FashionAndYou in September 2012. Her husband, Gaurav, had already left DealsandYou and Smile Group.

'The only thing I would change if I could do FashionAndYou again is to ensure I had at least 25 per cent stake in the company by Series C. I wouldn't be left with the kind of equity you give a senior hire to come on board.' She does not believe the common investor gyan that a company head's equity percentage makes no difference to the business and that the opportunity to build the business is what matters.

The gyan rang true in the early phase at FashionAndYou. Pearl was a star. FashionAndYou was a star. Whatever Pearl did turned to gold. But when the bad times came, she could do nothing right in the eyes of the investors.

These days Pearl and Gaurav take a long look at the capital table that entrepreneurs bring to Startup Superfuel. 'If you dilute so much at the seed funding stage, what will happen in Series A?' Pearl asks them. 'And once Series B happens, someone can get you out of the company without having to talk to you.'

In an investor-led company, entrepreneurs would never get complete freedom. But Pearl and Gaurav give their investee companies as much freedom as possible. 'If we think they are going in the wrong direction, we tell them. But if the founder says he knows what he is doing, we back him.' This approach is going to become more common as more and more entrepreneurs invest in others of their ilk.

Pearl hopes no one will have to go through the kind of exit she had to from FashionAndYou. For about six months before she quit, she was in two minds. What would she tell her team? It was a period of sheer agony. She wept the day she sent in her resignation. Pressing the send button for that email left her so distraught, she spent the next two hours driving around aimlessly, crying. She got off the car when her tears finally stopped, to find that all her stress, regret and pain had been washed away.

'I can look back with regret and think it could have been a billion dollar start-up, or a 10 billion dollar one. Or, I can look back the way I do, which is that I created value, I built something that others could build on.'

~

EPILOGUE

'*Tu* travel agent *banna chahta hai?*' (Do you want to be a travel agent?)

That is the angry retort Bhavish Aggarwal got from his father when he told him about his plans to set up his own company. 'Even though I am a bania from Ludhiana,' says Bhavish with a chuckle, when we meet at the OlaCabs' headquarters in Bangalore's Koramangala area, across the road from Sukh Sagar, a crowded sweet shop.

His chuckles are short and sharp, and make him look young, really young, and almost impish. With his shiny black hair covering the entire right side of his forehead, his slightly chubby cheeks and the little paunch pushing out from his T-shirt, he could still pass off as a student taking to devouring his mother's parathas while on vacation.

Both his parents are doctors. Bhavish went to IIT Bombay and joined Microsoft after graduating in 2008. He was in research; the nerd in him loved it. But you can hardly tie down a bania from Ludhiana in a job for very long. The community has always dominated commerce in this country, from ancient times to the modern era, and now has under its thumb a large chunk of the electronic commerce in the country. The Bahls, Bansals and Aggarwals you met in this book are all banias. And Ludhiana is known for its rich vein of

211

entrepreneurship that has thrown up the likes of Sunil Mittal and the Munjal family of the Hero Group.

So, two years of coding with Microsoft in Bangalore and Seattle, and Bhavish was done. He wanted to set up his own company, Olatrip.com. Based in Delhi, it was to sell weekend breaks and short-duration holidays online.

Bhavish's father was okay with his son trying his hand at business, but not with his becoming a 'travel agent'. He suggested that Bhavish get an MBA, work for some time, build a good, solid track record and then think of his own business. '*Abhi tumhe pata hi kya hai?*' he asked. (Whatever do you know now?)

He was correct. Bhavish did not know much. But he had a streak of adventure in him. 'You don't know what you don't know. I thought I knew everything.' In 2010, he left Microsoft and started Olatrip.com. The opportunity appeared immense. There were many popular weekend destinations to the north of Delhi in the Kumaon and Garhwal Himalayas, and to the west of the city, in Rajasthan.

The Commonwealth Games were happening that year. Thousands of visitors were going to throng Delhi. Naturally, they would want to take a bit of a break in the hills or desert when not watching the games.

Bhavish used to spend a lot of money on gadgets, and had saved only Rs 1 lakh from his two years at Microsoft. That was enough to start an online outfit that did not require much capital. He would stand outside the Commonwealth Games venues with a sheaf of pamphlets about the wondrous places that were just a short journey away.

'I did not sell a single trip,' he says. This time he does not chuckle, he laughs a hearty laugh.

He cut his losses, shut down Olatrip in four months and moved to Mumbai with an intriguing insight: People did want to take weekend breaks, but they did not want Bhavish to arrange all of it. They only wanted one part arranged: the vehicle. While trying to sell weekend holidays, he discovered he was getting many requests for cars. *'Nainital jana hai, yaar. Gaadi dila de.'* We are going to Nanital. Please get us a car.

So in Mumbai, Bhavish built a site for cars that could be hired for outstation trips. This he did with Ankit Bhati, who had graduated from IIT Bombay with an MTech in 2010. The new site was Olacabs.com. It would rent cars by the hour, or on a half-day or full-day basis. All done online.

The next logical move was to step into city cab services, of which there are so many now. Ola, alongside Uber, is fast becoming a generic name for cabs hired through a mobile app. In Bangalore especially, whenever I did a quick scan of the cars around me when stuck in traffic, I would observe that at least four out of ten cars were Olas.

Until recently, the company did not own any of the cabs. It was only in the middle of 2015 that it set up a subsidiary that would own cabs and give them to drivers on lease. Currently, an overwhelming majority of Ola cabs are owned by those who drive them. In my interactions with the drivers, I found them to be proud men. One of them berated me for shutting the door of his car with harder force than he thought appropriate.

Ola's growth was more or less parallel to Uber's rise overseas. It was the first of the taxi aggregators in India to launch a mobile app, way back in April–May 2012.

Bhavish had no background in business. 'One of the angels asked me for an "org chart"; I didn't know what it was.' So he built Ola from a fresh perspective and learned on the job, focusing only on the relevant and contextual, without any baggage of experience. 'We refined our model and vision. Right now, our vision is that people should not own cars.'

Bhavish does not own one. He uses Ola cabs three to four times a day, and gives frequent feedback as a customer.

Generally, the drivers do not know who they are ferrying. 'I don't feel the need to own a car—and that's what I am selling. A consumer business CEO should use his own product. I will not own a car ever.'

He has already prevailed upon his father-in-law to sell his car. This was the car he used to borrow from his wife, who was then his girlfriend, to pick up customers whenever there was no Ola cab available. Those were the days when he also managed the company's call centre. On occasion, he would take a call and say, 'Yes, sir, we will send the car.' And then, not finding anyone, drive down himself to pick up the customer.

In about seven to eight months of starting out, word spread that there was this new start-up trying to ease a pain point for people. A very small percentage of India's much-talked-about population owns cars. For many of those who do, parking is a daily struggle. Roads are congested. Hiring a driver costs a lot of money. Fuel costs were going up until 2014, when global crude oil prices began to fall. To top this all, the quality of public transport was abysmal. The folklore of Mumbai's local trains has no real music—ask anyone who uses them every day. Delhi's swanky metro is no better, despite the air-conditioning. Chennai's auto drivers have become living synonyms for nastiness. The situation is no better in Bangalore, Kolkata, Hyderabad, and so on.

Yet, everyone needs mobility. People need to go from one place to another.

'The solution is a platform like Ola's, where one car can serve ten people a day, instead of just one,' says Bhavish. 'Consumers need not worry about parking, maintenance, driver's salary, EMIs . . . Using Ola is cheaper.'

That's true. In many cases I have even found Ola to be on par with autorickshaws. By the way, autorickshaws are also now available on the Ola app.

With good word of mouth, the angels descended. Snapdeal's Kunal Bahl is an angel investor in Ola, apart from being a mentor and role model to Bhavish. Other angels include Anupam Mittal of shaadi.com. More organized funding came in the middle of 2012, when Ola raised Series A from Tiger Global. At the time, Ola was still doing only full and half-day rentals. The Series A money propelled it into city cab services.

Avnish Bajaj of Matrix came in during the next round in November 2013, and Sequoia stepped in with Series C in July 2014. SoftBank invested in October 2014. Today, Ola is the runaway leader among taxi aggregators.

It wasn't as easy as the paragraph above might suggest. It took cutting-edge technology, strong execution, a lot of hard work, and an unwavering focus on customer experience to win that eligibility.

'Raising the angel round was the toughest,' says Bhavish. 'The taxi business was not sexy. I was just a kid out of college. India was so not hot. E-commerce was going through a lean period.'

It did not help that Ola is not a purely online model. It involves cars and drivers, both needing to be dealt with offline. Given the nature of the business and its utility, demand was always strong. But finding the right kind of drivers, who could be trained to handle technology and serve the customer well, was a challenge. The government's concerns had to be taken care of; that is always a ticklish issue whenever a new industry launches.

Both Ola and Uber have had much regulation to traipse around, especially in Delhi, a large market, where an Uber cabbie raped a woman, triggering furore and a crackdown on taxi services.

But once Ola established a clear lead over the others, its momentum swept others out of its way, including the number two, TaxiForSure. Just before Bhavish and I met in March 2015, he had acquired TaxiForSure, which was at one point rising in a trajectory parallel to Ola's.

In an emerging business, the market and investors tend to veer towards the leader, especially if big investors bet their money on it. If SoftBank, Tiger and Matrix have already invested their money in Ola, betting on any of its rivals would mean betting against these big dudes. Few would do that.

The day we met, in fact, just an hour before we met, Ola had launched food delivery on its app. Bhavish says his youth—he is 1985 born—means nothing but a number, and that his mental age is very different. 'The last four years have felt like forty.' But he showed me the new food service on his phone with an endearing, childlike delight.

He also told me, with obvious pride and joy, that his mother in Ludhiana is now a regular Ola user. Earlier, his mother would have to wait for the family driver to return from the hospital after dropping off his father there. Sometimes she had to change her plans to accommodate her husband's schedule. Ola has set her free, as also their driver, who has now bought a car and joined the Ola network.

What does the father say now? Is he still upset his son became a 'travel agent'?

'He asks me when we will make money.'

The father is more attuned to traditional businesses, which do not leverage equity to grow. The tech opportunity is different. It is like a land-grab. You grow first, you make money later. Growth, by the way, is a limitless prospect for Ola. It is not confined to the taxi market, as its forays into autorickshaws and food as well. It is getting into shuttle services, where small buses will carry several commuters towards a common destination. That can be a blessing for local train commuters, such as those using the Delhi Metro, which has not solved the last-mile problem.

The true potential market for Ola is all mobility. Olacafé has shut down. But the day it was launched, Bhavish was very excited about it. His plan is to take Ola into all those services where a short delivery time is critical, such as in cabs.

'The opportunity for Ola,' says Bhavish, 'is all "on-demand" consumption.'

~

Vani Kola, who now runs Kalaari Capital, came to India in 2006 just to take a good look around at what was happening. She had been working in the United States since 1985, and had founded two companies in Silicon Valley, exiting both with sizeable financial gains. Her friends there included Vinod Dham, often called the father of the Pentium processor.

But Vani did not want to go on doing the same thing. She wanted to do something else, something more.

So in 2006, she sat in a mall in Gurgaon for five hours and observed. This mall was one of many on a single street, one shinier than the next. In the US, a mall was a place where you went to buy something and came back. But here she found that the mall was a place to eat out in, socialize, take the family for an evening out, etc.

Later, in Bangalore, she spoke to a taxi driver who was planning a trip to Bangkok. 'I work long hours, I have to keep the wife happy,' he said. 'I want to take her to a foreign country. Mahabalipuram won't do.'

This made Vani think about her father. Such a thought—that he had to do something special to make the wife happy—would not have crossed his mind. It was enough that he supported the family and was faithful.

She then visited a village on the outskirts of Bangalore where the sarpanch told her what a great thing it was that the village had a computer. She met a gardener in Bangalore who was proudly showing off a smart phone he had bought for an amount that equalled three times his monthly salary.

India had changed since she had left in 1985. It had become an aspirational, consumption-driven society. It was time to come back.

From the way Vani dresses, it would appear she was always meant to come back. Vani, who is in her early fifties, wears Indian ethnic chic on most days, with a nice little nose ring highlighting her face. The day we met, in a large conference room of Kalaari's office in Bangalore's Whitefield, she was wearing a bright necklace of beads she had bought online.

Her husband Srinivas, whom she had met while studying electrical engineering at Hyderabad's Osmania University, would have no problem with the shift to India. He had a boutique consulting outfit that focused on computer networking products and solutions. He could easily divide his time between India and the US.

Whatever doubts Vani may have had about her return were dispelled when her older daughter, twelve at the time, said: 'It will be a good adventure.'

Vani joined hands with Vinod Dham to start her first fund in India, IndoUS Venture Partners, in 2006. Five years later she started Kalaari, which is named after a Kerala martial art form.

Vani has quickly developed a name for making good picks: Snapdeal, Bluestone, Urban Ladder, Zivame, Apps Daily, and the one where she picked up that necklace of coloured beads from, Myntra, which is now in Flipkart's fold.

The secret to her success is simple. She first looks for a people connect. 'They need not be nice persons,' she says, 'but the intellectual connect is very, very important. Can I see deep insights and commitment? Has he brought something new to my thinking that intrigues me and excites me? Within that, can we have a productive work relationship?'

She works hard and wants to enjoy what she does. She also wants her investee company's founders to enjoy what they do. Energy should not be wasted in unnecessary friction.

The next important feature for a start-up would be its potential to take off and soar. When she met Mukesh Bansal, the founder of Myntra, she found him mature, reflective and introspective. Myntra's concept was solid, and held promise that consumer offtake would happen online, and that it was merely a matter of when. Mukesh was not bluffing; he was not trying to sell moonshine.

The same was true of Snapdeal's Kunal Bahl and Rohit Bansal. They showed deep insights into how they wanted to change demand aggregation for small and medium enterprises. They kept talking about the long-tail of demand in India. They understood its true power and potential. Small merchants could provide quality goods but could not have their products reach consumers. They needed a platform like Snapdeal.

It says something that Ratan Tata followed Vani into Snapdeal and Bluestone as an investor. He even joined Kalaari's advisory board.

India has also been good for Crea, Vani's Labrador. Born in 2000, she is still going strong. It appears that the constant company of people in India, and all the squirrel-chasing she gets to do here, has prolonged her life.

In the midst of this wholeness of life and career, Vani sometimes pauses to think about Ola and Bhavish. They had once spoken about Kalaari investing in Ola. Bhavish had seemed just the right type, and fulfilled both the criteria she likes in an entrepreneur: people-connect and potential to take off. 'We liked him a lot as CEO, thought he was a great guy. He excited us every time we interacted with him.'

But she was not sure how Ola would grow in a highly regulated country like India. That stopped her. 'There were many things he was doing right when we met him. But the cost of doing them was humungous, and the regulatory framework was a concern. We failed to see the momentum he could create.'

～

There is something about Bhavish. While Vani Kola wonders what might have been, Avnish Bajaj is glad he decided to bet on the young man. He too shared Vani's scepticism about Ola. He had doubts each time he looked at the market, which was chaotic, and wondered how Ola would ever make money. But Bajaj really liked Bhavish and decided to work with him.

That something, which makes Bhavish a darling of investors, is the same magic quality that makes Flipkart, Snapdeal, Paytm, Practo, Stayzilla, ShopClues, LimeRoad, Mu Sigma, and some others like them so precious. They are committed to solving a problem that is a royal pain you-know-where for a large section of the population.

The happy side effect of these entrepreneurs solving their chosen problems is that they are also addressing the country's biggest problem: lack of jobs. About a million people join the workforce every month. There are not enough jobs to accommodate them because India moved swiftly from an agrarian economy to a services economy, skipping the stage of manufacturing, which is the sector that creates a large number of jobs. No wonder the government is trying to do its bit, without great success so far, to encourage entrepreneurs, who are job creators and not jobseekers.

The special something about successful entrepreneurs is that they think 'scale' with a sense of entitlement because they have thought things through. They are also at the right place at the right time, with the right focus and employ strong execution.

The formula works.

In July 2014, Nikesh Arora, who had left Google where he was head of global sales, was on a four-week break for his marriage to Ayesha Thapar. Masayoshi Son, the head of SoftBank who is globally acknowledged as a whiz for his investments in telecom and Internet, had hired Nikesh as president, but Nikesh was yet to join SoftBank.

Still, Masa called Nikesh and asked if he could do something about Kunal Bahl. SoftBank wanted to buy half of Snapdeal, but Bahl was not biting. Nikesh stepped in and eventually SoftBank was able to buy a little over 30 per cent of Snapdeal.

Nikesh did not stop there. He had no office, but had two mobile phones with which he worked out of the backseat of a car, connecting with several other entrepreneurs looking for funds. When Sunil Mittal, whom Nikesh has known for a while, agreed to lend him space in his office in New Delhi's Vasant Kunj, Nikesh met forty entrepreneurs there in the space of two days. One of them was twenty-one-year-old Ritesh Agarwal of OYO Rooms, who got SoftBank's money.

A little later, Nikesh ran into Bhavish and flew him down to Tokyo to meet Masa. They had dinner. The next morning, they had a deal. SoftBank would invest $210 million in Ola.

∼

SoftBank's entry is a high-water mark for the Indian start-up scene. It signs fewer cheques as compared to other funders, but makes them large. It makes its picks after observing which way the market is going, and hardly ever invests in more than one company in a segment. It invests proprietary money, not funds raised from LPs, or limited partners, as other fund houses do. Its investments are therefore seen as seriously accountable. For example, SoftBank's investment in Ola may have turned the sentiment away from the challenger TaxiForSure, and tipped the scales firmly in Ola's favour.

In many ways, therefore, SoftBank's arrival marks a sort of maturing of the ecosystem, which barely existed a decade ago. Earlier, there were higher odds stacked against start-ups. So, few young people turned entrepreneur. You would remember, from the previous chapters, Phanindra Sama's travails when he did not really know what to do with redBus. Bus operators did not want its software. Sama stumbled on to TiE and Sanjay Anandaram stepped in as mentor. That changed redBus's course.

Today's entrepreneurs do not really need to rely on serendipity (which, by definition, cannot be relied on). When I had met Sanjay, he explained this indicator as the third wave of entrepreneurship in India.

The first wave consisted of the old-world, pre-liberalization, licence-seeking guys who looked at India as a market. The second, the information technology and BPO fellows, looked at India as a launch pad, but searched for and found their markets overseas. The third wave, the current one, is again building businesses for India but in concept, execution, and ambition, the businesses can hold their own against any in the world.

Of the several companies Sanjay has mentored, he finds redBus the most interesting. It was set up by true techies who had nothing to do with the Internet; they taught themselves the Internet by reading books. They had no background in business, no family heritage. And they wanted to solve a problem they had experienced.

'The most interesting businesses are where the market is amorphous, and the players in that market are trying to understand what is happening.' The bus industry was like that when redBus started: disorganized, fragmented, unsophisticated, yet sanguine in the belief that it had worked for half a century and would continue to work the same way, regardless of all the problems faced by the end consumer.

The evolution of the Indian entrepreneur has been helped along by the advancement of the funding scenario. When the tech bubble burst in 2000–01, both entrepreneurship and funding had been fairly wiped out.

At the time Sanjay decided to hand-hold redBus, his own Jumpstartup was one of the rare Silicon Valley-style funds operating in India. However, as the third phase of entrepreneurship began to come of age, more and more of funds came to India and set up busy shops here.

There is another quiet revolution taking place in this area: the rise of angels.

~

Renu Malik began to cry.

A gynaecologist, she had married a paediatrician. Not only that, thirty-seven of her husband's cousins were doctors. Renu had sent her only son, Ritesh, to Theni, a small place in Tamil Nadu, to do his MBBS. And now he was saying he would not be a doctor. Worse, he wanted to join a start-up.

A few months later, in 2013, all the doctors in the extended Malik family were rejoicing. Ritesh's start-up, Adstuck, had earned a tidy sum for its first app.

Using his share of the money, Malik became an angel: a person who invests in the early stages of a start-up when the big fund houses won't give them the time of day.

Ritesh not only gives them the time of day but also a room in the hotel his family owns in East Delhi. At twenty-six, he has already funded twenty companies. He is one of several from myriad backgrounds who do so. They are not the run-of-the-mill technology entrepreneurs investing in technology start-ups. They are the unusual angels.

Robin Uthappa is never too far from the Indian cricket team. He is never too far from a kitchen either, cooking frequently at home or telling the chefs at restaurants to customize his order. He put in Rs 1.5 crore as the first investor in iTiffin, a Bangalore-based online service that delivers nutritious meals to the customer's doorstep. 'Robin also helps us design meals and reach the right audience,' says Tapan Das, iTiffin's co-founder.

Shravan Shroff owned and ran the Fame cinemas until 2011, when he sold them to INOX for Rs 65 crore. He has put 10 per cent of that money in thirty start-ups. One of those was ZipDial, known for its service that connects brands with consumers through missed calls. Twitter bought it in January this year for a reported $30 million. Shroff stays invested in OYO Rooms, a network of hotels online and offline, that is receiving high valuations.

Then there is Ravi Kiran who finds angel investing the best way to learn. Kiran was a top executive with advertising and media buying firms for twenty years until 2010, when on his way to Cannes, he ran into Sasha Mirchandani of Mumbai Angels at Paris airport. Mirchandani asked Kiran if he could help a start-up understand the mindset of media buyers. Kiran did, and was hooked. He has invested Rs 5 to Rs 10 lakh each in more than two dozen start-ups.

Rajesh Krishnan was with Lehman Brothers when it collapsed in September 2008. He moved to Nomura, which bought Lehman Asia, and on to Standard Chartered from there.

Even as the financial world shook, real estate was making money. In 2011, Krishnan left his job to set up Brick Eagle, which does affordable housing. He has gone on to invest in a number of start-ups, all pursuing activities in affordable housing: TPC (construction technology), Xeco (branding and marketing), Phalcomm (online platform to sell houses), Foyr (online interior designer), and Botsworth (robotics for township management).

Many of these angels continue to do other things. Krishnan runs Brick Eagle. Kiran works as a management consultant. Shroff has a large portfolio of stocks and bonds. Uthappa plays cricket. And Ritesh Malik, last November, started his second start-up, a co-working space company named Innov8, which is spreading rapidly to Chandigarh, Mumbai and Bangalore.

And then there is the 1937-born Ratan Naval Tata. Having retired as chairman of Tata Sons in 2012, he has emerged as a great backer of young entrepreneurs. Apparently, all it takes to make him invest in your start-up is to ask him, goes the lore.

According to reports, Nidhi Agarwal's Kaaryah was rejected by 113 investors before she, at her father's suggestion, found Ratan Tata's email ID and wrote to him. And Tata decided to invest in her venture.

Maybe fairy tales do happen. But it will not be wise to count on them. If you are serious about getting Tata, you should go through every line of what he said at the 2015 convocation of Great Lakes Management Institute in Chennai. Here is the gist.

'You must not come across as someone chasing valuations, you ought to have a sense of responsibility'. Linked to that is commitment. And passion. Tata gets impressed by those who have good ideas and no support, but great passion to achieve what they do.

Tata prefers those that help improve the common man's life, typically ideas related to health, empowerment of women, access to the Internet, and the like.

He has invested in Snapdeal, which gives access to all kinds of goods to all kinds of people in all kinds of places—sellers as well as buyers; in Ola, which solves an everyday problem for those who live in cities with bad public transport—which is nearly every city in India; in wind energy company, Altaeros, (actually his first investment in a start-up); and Coimbatore-based electric bikes maker Ampere.

Agarwal's Kaaryah is an interesting case. It sells a blend of western and Indian formal clothing for women in eighteen different sizes—the usual being six—which accommodate the different body proportions found among Indian women, addressing issues like gaping buttons on shirts. These creative types usually face the problem of financial support, because their concept often appears vague and esoteric. Tata finds it important to nurture and support them.

Of course, the start-ups receiving Tata's money benefit in more than one way. The buzz has it that investor interest and valuations shoot up. The founder of a public relations firm told me she was kicking herself for letting go of a start-up client that went on to receive Tata's money. The journalists she used to chase earlier were now chasing her to talk to the founder of that start-up. And she had been apologizing saying they no longer worked together.

That's not all. All the modern, successful entrepreneurs are funding a raft of start-ups. When Sachin Bansal, Binny Bansal, Kunal Bahl, Vijay Shekhar Sharma, Phanindra Sama and others are not running their companies or raising funds for them, they are blooding and hand-holding other entrepreneurs. But it could not be called a revolution if new-age angel-investing was limited to them.

~

There are times, though, when things do not work out despite everything being right or appearing so.

The subject of Rahul Yadav inevitably arose when Nikesh Arora, SoftBank's President and COO, came to *Mint* newspaper's office in October 2015, a meeting to which I was fortunately invited.

We raised the subject gingerly. Is the youth of today's entrepreneurs a problem for investors, many of whom are seasoned professionals?

'When I was young I thought all the old people were not smart enough. Now that I am old, I think the young people are not mature enough,' said Nikesh, who is 1968-born. 'From my interactions with entrepreneurs, I would say that maturity and age do not have a direct correlation.'

Then he came to the point.

When Nikesh first met Rahul, he found him to be different, refreshingly so, from the other entrepreneurs. He said the housing space was about creating great products for the end customer; it was not about listings and trying to sell. Housing.com stood out for being product-centric, as opposed to business-centric.

Nikesh fully agreed with Rahul. And that meant that the first criterion for funding was met. Any investor likes alignment with the fundamental problem that the entrepreneur is trying to solve. Is it worth solving? Will the business find a market? If the answers are yes, the rest, in the early stage of a venture, is mere detail.

'We had that alignment,' said Nikesh. 'The part we had not bargained for is that he has a personality that overwhelmed the company. He can be erratic at times. And that's something you discover only after you have interacted with him over a period of time. We had not seen that earlier.'

Last heard, Rahul was asking his thousands of followers on Facebook whether he should give up entrepreneurship and take up a job. That was just after he tried to work with the government on a virtual reality project to improve efficiency.

Things did not go to plan. He has also spoken to other entrepreneurs, one of them Paytm founder Vijay Shekhar Sharma, for investing in his venture. Rahul does not want to ride the tiger of investor money again.

As Yadav left Housing.com and the company lost its early lustre, the fortunes of SoftBank's other investments in India did not exactly soar. There have been questions about the health of Snapdeal and InMobi. Ola has run into Uber, one of the biggest start-up successes in the world, and is calling it a foreign company that does not respect Indian laws. OYO, a marketplace for budget hotels, has to contend with Airbnb, and its acquisition of ZO Rooms appears to be less than triumphant.

But it was Yadav whom people sought out when Nikesh Arora resigned as president of SoftBank on 21 June 2016. The day before, an internal probe had cleared Nikesh of charges of conflict of interest—because he was also an investor to private equity firm Silver Lake—levied by a group of unnamed SoftBank investors. These investors had also likened Nikesh's investment strategy to throwing a dart at a dartboard.

On Twitter, Arora tried to impart dignity to the proceedings by saying he was sure Yadav had better things to do than track Arora's life.

He was wrong. 'Well, Nikesh, I'm very much *lukkha* these days,' Yadav posted on Facebook. Lukkha is Hindi for total slacker. In this case, it also refers to a person who loves a scrap, against whom you cannot win.

~

INDEX